Forged into Authenticity
An Anthology

By
Crystal M. Gaines

© Copyright 2017 – Crystal Marie Gaines

The poetry and writings in this book are the original work of Crystal Marie Gaines, with all rights reserved, except where other content used is acknowledged. Scriptures used are from The Holy Bible, King James and Easy to Read Versions, respectively. No part of this book may be reproduced or transmitted in any form or by any means, electronic or mechanical, including photocopying, recording or by any information storage and retrieval system without written permission from the author with an allowance being made only for brief excerpts to be used in reviews.

CryGain Publishing House, LLC
15306 S. Robey Avenue
Harvey, IL 60426

ISBN 978-0-692-85343-6

For Worldwide Distribution
Printed in the U.S.A.

THE JOURNEY

Preface 7
Acknowledgements 9
The Reason 13
Recovery Unto the Will of God 17
Overeater's Anonymous 19
Let Me Teach You Love 23
To The Men I've Known 27
If Men Are Like Buses 29
A Life Defined... For Now 32
The School of Life 36
If You Only Knew 39
The Evil of Opened Eyes (aka opin-i-ons) 43
I Miss My Child 48
Happy Mother's Day? 53
Jesus is That Kind of Place 57
Note to my Younger Self 59
The Reintroduction to Me 60
I Rise 64
In Love 66
For Real – The Prelude: 68
For Real 68

The Truth of Imperfection 70
The Mask I Won't Wear 72
Through the eyes of a child on behalf of children and their parents.. 75
For Mom. (On Mother's Day).. 77
Let Go.. 79
Love's Honesty 82
Go Through 85
Closure -- The Right Way 89
Is THIS Love? 92
A Letter to My Long-Lost Love.. 96
My National Boyfriend Day poem 100
Let me tell you about A Woman of God 103
Sittin' -- Reflections as I Unwind 106
Twenty-One (...Again).. 112
The Way Of Love 114
My Father's Thoughts to me 116
My Close-Out Customer Service Policy from 1960 to Now 117
On the Night Before New Year's.. 119
My Closeout List of Gratitude.. 121
A Tree Just for Me 124
Expression in Spanish.. 128
My perspective on Why did I Get Married, Too" 129
About Friendship 132
About Love & Truth.. 133

To Jesus, With Love 137

My Heart's Cry – For Truth 139

Whatever happened to... 142

Impossible: A job for Superman 146

My Heart's Cry – For Wisdom...150

The Demand to a Risen Savior from a Wounded Soul 154

Love Loves the Prodigal One...159

It Happened One Night 162

Your Face of Grace..165

The Arrival 167

Believe Again 169

Love in the Dance 172

♥ *Thank you for reading about my journey from darkness to Light* ♥

Preface

When I was thinking about a title, a forged heart was what came to me. I was thinking about a heart shaped by fire and molded by pain and heat. But when I looked up the word **forged**, I found a different, but more accurate meaning: *a forged instrument*, in other words, *a forgery*, which I learned that even having one is a crime that could land you in Federal prison for many years. Then I thought about my life and the path that I was on B.C., Before Christ. I was a forger. In other words, a forgery. Because I didn't know who I was.

A journey is a pathway that begins with the first step. There is usually a goal in taking that journey, a place that you want to end up. I remember my journey, which begun at Word of Faith Fellowship in Chicago, IL in July of 1989. I had nothing. I was nothing. I was in severe pain and barely hanging onto my life. I became a forgery. I became what everyone thought I should be. I was a chameleon. Changing into whatever someone wanted me to be, because all I wanted, was just to be-long to someone, until Christ, through my pastor, caught and captured the real me. And then, the forging of my soul began, a forging into authenticity.

This book is a snapshot of that journey.

Acknowledgements

I want to thank my Pastor, Dr. Rickey Singleton, for being willing to take me in to his ministry and into the family of God. The man of God who was and still is God's anvil, laboring hard over me, praying and working relentlessly on me in the state I was in. Thank you for allowing God to pour His love into me through your voice, breathing into me the will to live. Instilling into me the courage to let go of all of that internal shrapnel lodged in my heart and taught me how to accept that I belonged to God and beloved by Him, too. And then... worked tirelessly with me, even when I didn't believe in myself, not only where I can write, but now I can write for others and publish their books, too.

I also want to thank those who caused me pain from childhood until now. For if you had not rejected and abandoned me, bullied and made fun of me, pulling the rug out from under me over and over again, I would have never become empty enough to discover that underneath my bottomless pit was the everlasting love of Jesus Christ and that it was there all along. I want to thank my teachers, Mr. Alan Rubens, who showed me that I was NOT dumb, but actually smart and to Mr. Larry Shapiro, who awakened the gift of writing in me, when I couldn't find the voice to scream loud enough, you gave me a voice to write out of my agony and unknowingly preserved my life. I want to thank my grandmother, who loved and buffered me from the brunt of constant hate. I also want to thank my mother, through you, I have learned that life can be raised out of death.

I thank my friend, writing-sister and editor, Lawana Spearmon-Lee. One who has loved me unconditionally and who encouraged me to put my poetry life into a message that hopefully will help someone else make it through.

Finally, this is for my Jesus. My Lord. My Rescuer. The Lover and Restorer of my soul. Without you, none of this would exist because I would not exist. You are my First, my Last, my Everything. Without You, I would simply dissolve, for you are my Core. Everything I am comes from You. It was You Who defined me in the beginning, as a father defines his child when they are born. You continually fill me full of everything You are and I am your happy and willing container ready to pour Your love out upon the world.

I love you Jesus, more than anything.

Crystal

"*Then I went down to the potter's house, and, behold, he wrought a work on the wheels. And the vessel that he made of clay was marred in the hand of the potter: so he made it again another vessel, as seemed good to the potter to make it.*"

Jeremiah 18:3-4 KJV

The Reason

I close my eyes
Not expecting to be alive
But I am
The pain intense
Thinking that this is the end
But it's not
I close my heart in sleep and silently pray
Lord, please take me away
But He doesn't
Been sucker punched
Exposed to the elements
And yet,
I still stand
Because I have a job to do

When I think I've had enough
Life gets hard
And I feel like giving up
SomeOne holds me together
And in spite of me, every day's another chance.

I'm alive for a reason
In spite of fire so intense before me
only for a moment it'll last
for I know I've got a right to be here

Because He loves me
I am not my own
I'm bought with a price

Too precious to die
Won't let go
Because I know that He loves me
And He is the reason I live

My soul's been fried
because of the trials of fire I've walked through
plunged into waters of my own tears, so deep
I thought I'd drown, I've cried so much
But by His power I'm still afloat
as I see Him turn them all into wells of blessing
the raft of His great faithfulness
keeps me moving forward
When I didn't think I could take another step
or thought I'd never breathe again,
somehow I do
'cause deep within my heart,
I know He's won
The battle for my soul was completed
Before the day I was born
Now it's mine mandate to make that life real on earth

So in the darkest night
as I awake to a new day
I join in with my Heavenly Father's Voice
and sing the song I hear…
I'm alive for a reason
In spite of fire so intense before me
only for a moment it'll last
for I know I've got a right to be here

Because He loves me

I am not my own
I'm bought with a price
Too precious to die
Won't let go
Because I know that He loves me
And He is the reason I live
So giving up is not an option
Gotta keep on moving forward
because His Love toward me's true
and I've got a job to do

All that I am He is
all That He is, I am
and He is the reason I live
He is the reason I live

Though the winds strong and mighty may come
And the rains of fiery accusations may dash against me
my confidence may be torn and shipwrecked
on the billows of opinion and true bad mistakes
yet on the solid rock of Christ
I stand surrendered and upheld by His amazing grace
It's not my will, but His, for my life, to be done
And if it is to die
it's only to die to my own way
and arise to live again this day
and another and another and yet another
Alive for Him, to worship Him, my call
Doing things His way from now on
Because He loves me
I am not my own

I'm bought with a price
Too precious to die
Won't let go
Because I know that He loves me
And He is the reason I live
So giving up is not an option
Gotta keep on moving forward
because His Love toward me's true
and I've got a job to do
All that I am He is
all That He is, I am
and He is the reason I live
He is the reason I live

Recovery Unto the Will of God

I am recovering
from pretense and mediocrity
Putting aside the need to be
street slick and a dollar short to get my way
And I am putting aside all of my childish ways
Living in codependency what would be the point?
I'm not determining my life or worth
On other people's opinion about who I should be
or how I should look
I made the decision to live who I AM
Unapologetically, I cast my life
In the Arms of my Master, My closest and dearest Friend
Taking a bold leap into His Arms once again.
Regaining my focus, leaving my past behind, Breaking out,
coming out mightily
Jettisoning all of the offspring I bore out of a life now past
away
I let them go freely to fly on their own
And live lives on the path that THEY chose
While as for me and the house that God has for me
I've chosen to walk in agreement and peace with my life's
plan from God

Like an eagle renewing itself sheds it feathers
Breaks off its own beak, not to die, but to be reborn
I undergo my own transition,
From out of my strength into that
which comes from God alone

To align my life choices
with the will and plan of my Father God
I am now airborne
into renewed strength, renewed youth
completing my mission with new fervor
fulfilling my assignment in the Earth
through His supernatural Power
My DNA changed into His divine nature
Out of the realm of hate, I'm bathed into His Love
And through the power of that transformation
I experience eternal life now in this time
And live on and on and on.
Reaping the rewards I really want -- Eternally
more abundantly
Naturally. Authentically, all of me
My life on exhibition in the name of Jesus my Christ
Amen and So Be it.

As sure as the promises of God
Here I am, Lord
Send me.

Overeater's Anonymous

I'm eating
Because I'm pissed off
at the way you think you can talk to me, and it's okay
it's always OK...'cause nobody stops you
cause right is on your side,
the evidence you have against me outweighs your good sense
Because you are so special
And I to you am nothing.
But I know better...

Because I am no less than you
We both belong to the SAME God
And are BOTH justified
By the SAME blood

So how, Lord Jesus???
How do I stop being angry
With this one, the one so much older than I
(the one who is so much better...)
And what you say, and how you say it
(Intimidating me, all in my face,
Like I'd better listen)
How do I keep from walking away,
(Who the hell do you think I am??)
How I want to so badly
(But LORD where would I go??)

But I can't (How can I walk away)
because I LOVE The LORD.

(From the One Who loves me so)
He heard my cry
And pities every groan
(So my soul lays silent before Him…)
I love Him so

And this is why, I hold my peace
And silently sit and process this
This is why walk away and haven't cussed you out
For respect of Him I don't just tell you really 'bout yourself
What would be the point?
You won't believe me, if I did
Cause of what you THINK you know about me

But you're assuming that I am deserving of less
(other than my place in Him through the Blood of Jesus and
MY inheritance
through His righteousness)
You've got another thing comin', Miss.

I suppose it's my fault.
It took me longer to get the point
To mature and accept the responsibility for my decisions
I give you that
But your acidic bitter ways
Surely don't make you any better
Than my "wretched" "miserable" self
You just appear so
Because you can hide your poison behind a smile
Your poverty, behind the multitude of temporal things.
But I cannot do it anymore.
I'm open.

Exposed in wide eyed view
So I guess because you see my faults
you think you've got one up on me
And you most likely do
But with me, My God ain't through
It ain't over, because I'm still breathing
And every day, for me God's got something new
So after you've done your best
Kicked the dust and walked away
I'll get back up in the name of my Victor,
dust myself off and go to bat once again,
And again, and again and again and again
Until... I ... WIN!

And maybe, I'll hit a home run just for you.

In the meantime, I need to sit
In this corner, recovering
Working it out between me and Jesus
Crying out before Him
To change me and repair my perception
Wipe the mud out of my eyes
So I can change my attitude
From one of anger to one yielded to the Prince of Peace
I need my spirit protected and shielded
While my heart recovers from this bruise
So that it's Him (not me) that's in view
When you come back to examine me... again
Is she dead? Hell, NO!

So, help me, Dear Jesus

Give ear unto MY cry
As I've eaten dinner, lunch and two bagels
I know that this is not the answer:
Eating and ingesting the fight that I feel
When what I really want to do, right now
Is beat the shit out of a punching bag
like a heavyweight boxer
Cause I am too chicken to take it out on the one
Who really thinks they've got it ALL together.

I don't see how, if you're hating on me.
But I know that's not the way I ought to be
So now, I plead on bended knee…

Cleanse me.
Wash me.
Reach me where I am.
My childhood is forever GONE
I'll NEVER be a child again

So now being the woman I am
I want to be a better one
—better than I was when I began.

Let Me Teach You Love

I wrote this song (YES, it's my very first song!!!) because, I felt the need to express my heart to someone special. A lot of times, when we fall for someone, we expect them to be perfect. with no flaws at all, when WE are not even that way ourselves. We disappoint. We hurt. and We let others down. ALL the time. Those who love us and depend on us the most are the ones who can truly tell the story of our imperfections. But we, in our search for self-perfection, fail to listen. It saddens me that we are so quick to hold imperfect people to such a high standard, and then give up on them when they don't measure up.

Our marriages and families are wounded crushed and are breaking up because we do not see the opportunities to sow the things we want to see into the people that enter into our lives. We're so quick to judge and throw them away, only to find out later that they actually were the prize. I can't do that anymore. Not with myself nor with anyone else. For I am born of LOVE and I am born to love... and to love is NOT to have to have sex.

Love bears up under anything and everything that comes, is ever ready to believe the best of every person, its hopes are fadeless under all circumstances, and it endures everything [without weakening].
1 Cor 13:7 AMP

I.

How could I have known when I met you
When I looked into your eyes and saw you smile
That I'd fall so hard when I wasn't even looking
That my heart would opened up when I wasn't expecting
anything at all

How could I have guessed that time
you put your arm around me
And on the bus you kissed my forehead tenderly
Caressed my eyes with just one look
And kissed my lips so gently
That I'd sigh because I knew
my heart had fallen for you
From that point on
from that point on
You were just another person sitting by me
I wasn't expecting you to reach out to me that day
but I looked beyond the present moment
And did something, before I'd never would
I took a chance to see beyond myself
and I saw you

But a romance for just one night
isn't what I'm looking for
I believe within my heart,
with you there's so much more
And if you'll take this journey with me
In time you'll see I'm right
If you'll take the time
Let's take the time

Chorus:
Let me teach you love
A love that will last
A love that most miss
Because they go in too fast

Let me teach you right
Not just for one night
Let me give you gifts
That'll last for all time
Let me teach you love
My love
Let me teach you love.

II.
Love is just so easy to say nowdays
People come your way
What sweet things do they say
Promise you the world, for a cheap and easy thrill
They take the best you have to give
then they leave you alone
a little less of you each time than you were before
pickin' up the shattered pieces of your broken heart
leaving you with nothing
as they take all your money too
as your hope to find a real love, slowly dies

But I want a love that I won't regret
When comes the morning dawn
Within this thing we'll both be smiling
Cause we make each other strong
And if in loving you, I can't increase your life
Then let's move on

You've been broken before
Don't want to break you down no more

For there is so much more to life
than just a horizontal dance
But something real and lasting is what we can have
So let me teach you love
like you've never had before
Let's do that thing very few have done
and for us, write a different song

Let me teach you love.

(Yeah, RIGHT!)

To The Men I've Known

Had to expel you from my passion
Release you into the Winds of destiny
I loved you and wanted the very best for you
But that I cannot want, more than you do.

I want you happy
But cannot make you choose the good
That will bring you real and lasting peace
Only the Lord of Love can empower you to reach for that
If only you would choose
To take that step into that place of Grace
And discover the power to break free
of that which you say you're tired of
instead of falling for that same ole song
But I cannot take that step for you
For I am not your mother
And I am no one's sometime lover
To have to listen while you complain
of something you are truly not completely done with
because you give into it over and over again

I am a woman of God.
And I'm looking for a city
Which has a foundation
Whose builder and maker is my Father God.
How can you love me
When you cannot even love yourself?

How can you want me
When you won't even accept that
Which will empower you to heal yourself?
I told you when I met you
That I have no time for games
And yet, though I feel deep things for you
I will not walk in the muck of your choosing with you
The thing that you have settled for your life
Is not the thing I need in mine
For I am not your pastime paradise
Nor will I become a friend with benefits
that I know I will not benefit from
'cause recreational lovin's not what I'm after
Even though that's all you seem to bring.
I am a woman of God.
And I'm waiting for a man
Who has a foundation
Whose builder and maker is God.

If Men Are Like Buses

If men are like buses...
If men are like buses, and if you miss one
another one will come every 25 minutes onto your path
Let's look at the commute, shall we?

If when you catch a bus, you're supposed to
a: know where you are
and b: know where you want to go
and then c: you need to know how to get there.

Now, you can get there several ways;
1. you could go the direct route
2. you could (if you have the time) take a more scenic route
or 3. (in case of emergencies or unforeseen detours)
you should always have a backup plan.
and leave in enough time for contingencies

So, if men are like buses
should you not already;
a: know where you are, more like WHO you are
b: know where you want to go,
in other words, what your path of purpose is
and c: you need to know how you're going to get there
at the least know what the next step you need to take
then you'll have an idea as to
who should be your partner to help you get there? yes?

So if you're a woman, who knows these things
and you have your purpose in hand

and you're on the right plan,
doing that thing only you can do
if it's not supposed to be up to you to choose
for the man, he's supposed to pick you, right?

if you're on the RIGHT path
how did the wrong bus come your way?

if you were expecting the right one
and you got on the bus that came your way, thinking
I'm finally on my way home
but found out that the bus driver was only taking a shortcut
and thought you wanted an express bus,
'cause he thought all you were worth was only a booty call?

HEY!! stop this bus and let me off!   NOW!!!

So if you are a woman
with purpose in your hand
you're on a mission for God
but the job before you, it's bigger than you
don't be jaded and don't be rude
you can't keep pushing away your miracle
don't be used to letting these buses pass you by
people say

so how do you know it's safe to board the next bus
approaching you
when it's not supposed to be up to you
if it's the man who's supposed to be choosing you?
then how the hell did this happen to you?
your heart is not for sale

Yet, once again you find yourself in a place
that is no longer safe, Huh?
So now you've gotten off "the bus"
and you are pissed because now you have to walk back
to the place of singular focus
(the stop) you were at before
(DAMN)
and you still have to wait on the "right" bus
'cause you still need to get home
(more time missed recovering over this one.)

So if men are like buses
and you're on the right path
don't all buses look the same?
If I read the sign that said, "my destination"
How in the world did I end up being wrong
So how DO you keep from getting on the buses
that detour you emotionally
driving you some place you didn't ask to go
that leave you stranded, saying
How in the hell do I get home?
It's not my Father I don't trust
it's these buses.
why should I "get on the bus, leave the driving to us"
when you don't even know where I'm going
cause you're so busy lusting after my pocket change
at the expense of my full cost.

skip this commute, Get me a car.

A Life Defined… For Now

I am.
In spite of me, I exist.
I am Crystal and I'm still here.
Approaching maturity at the altitude of grace.
Coming in for a landing in a peaceful place
I'd never thought I'd see,
yet, thanks to The Lord, I'm here.

To all the ones I've loved and lost, no hard feelings to you.
For in your own way, you contributed to my development
I now know what I don't want.
For those who God has removed from my life,
it's all for the best.
The scars you've left behind now shine as testaments of His
glory of redeeming me from what you thought I would be.
It matters not to me anymore what you think I was,
if I've changed or not, you'll never see it if I did, because you
are not looking for any of the right reasons.
I am free. No longer enslaved, nor held captive by
the need for your approval.
I am hopeful. Expecting my life to be for the best
A better being I am now
because I am for the first time in my life, alive in my own
skin.
I am alive, by His Mighty Power.
No more do I exist because you said so.
No more seeking sex from a johnnycomenever
as a sloppy substitute for love
(you never could come right, if you know what I mean…)
For you added nothing to my life
but a waste of my time and talent

(yes, I said it, 'cause it's true)

Unaware of my value, I let you walk all over me.
I took your stripes of anger and selfishness
I bowed to what I thought I had to accept
But no more. Tonight is the night that I close the door.
I'm approaching the best of my life at the altitude of blessing
Your opposition only fuels my ascension
And there is NOTHING you can take away from me.

I am free and I walk on
jettisoning the cargo of the foundational years of my life
I cast off from my distressed ship
the heavy weight of your misguided expectations.
It don't matter anymore.
I gave it all to Jesus
shipping the broken down cargo and dead weight of my pain
to lighten my heart for the new
embracing the next fifty years of my life

as an adventure brand new
A heavenly set up just for me
To define for the world, by his Word
just who I am -- Anointed
For I am that I am -- Appointed
in his name, ALIVE. – and I'm on it!

My life now being defined only
By the One who created it.
And He never makes a mistake.

When He made me He broke the mold
And destroyed your yoke
Because of His Anointing

on the one who He chose to save my life

and destroy forever the doors to prisons
that I lived in for so long
Never thought I belong anywhere else.
But now I have a new home
A place I don't have to run and hide
Nor compromise my heart and life
Nor body, just for the gravel of this world's lustful gain
For He knows me as I fully am, all my ins and outs,
My weaknesses, faults, and frailties
do not shock nor surprise Him
Whether or not I have changed, doesn't matter
For He loves me just the same.
I live, I move and I have my being,
In His Mighty and Majestic Name.
His love supersedes all expectations
His life is now within my heart
And if there is or if there never will be

one who comes to love me
He is... and will forever be
The Lover and Protector of my heart.

So I am cruising toward Fifty
Flying high toward my destination
Of obediently fulfilling my purpose
by the Power of His Grace
That's the way I am to be
Flowing full speed ahead to see what the end's going to be
No matter how many grey hairs frame my face
It is lovely because my face is aglow with His love
And my heart burns anew
Bright with the flame of His Amazing Love.

And the next years of my life's story
Will never be the same.

Just keep on watching…
For I am a miracle happening right before your eyes.
And let the haters say, Amen.

The School of Life

Life is.
Hard, when you haven't learned to listen
Even harder when you haven't been taught.
The hardest, when you insist on doing things your own way
Handling life in the way that you know
Haven't you learned that that's not going to work?
Because there is always someone who knows more than you.
And that someone is God
All wrapped up in packages of His own choosing,
These are His lessons
In wrappings that don't always look, sound or feel so good
But end up being the best thing for you
If you endure the class they assign to you

For ditching the school of life is not option
Especially when you become "grown"
If you learn early, then your later life is a rest
If not, the repeats that are repeated the more they are repeated
are costlier and more "devastating"
than the simple test itself
(Remember, Pete and Repeat were sitting on the desk,
Pete fell off, so who was left? Re-peat...
Well, why be that kind of fool?)

Life is... a bitch, if you fight the process
A bust... when you fall down, hard
A blessing... when you learn the lessons
that honestly could not be taught any other way

And becomes full bloom, as you surrender
after God, through His word, gets through with you
And a basketcase for those who refuse to heed or listen
But, again, I ask (first myself) why be that kind of fool?

When life as designed by God was meant to be
Full, bountiful and free?
It is us in this life, by our carnal "over-thinking"
who make things way more complicated
than they really have to be
and by our religious "over-praying",
we don't tend to the things that are necessary
to bring about the solution
that we've told God that we need

The lessons we have to walk through then
Take more time to break in
beyond our hard head cranium cavity,
just to get into our broken heart
and speak until we realize that God… is God
And we… are simply not.

*Jesus Christ is Lord,
means so much more than what we've been taught.
Even though we think we've heard it all before
Our lives display that we haven't heard much
Perhaps life itself is trying to tell us something
and here's what that something is…
that we need to shut up and hear some more.
Until we truly get it.*

At least that's what it taught me.

If You Only Knew

If you only knew what it's like to be a parent
You'd watch the things you say as a child, 'bout yours
If you knew what it was like to see
Your baby boy or girl be born/as seen with your own eyes
as they come out of your body
both of you are crying in the night
not knowing when your next meal was coming from
And then see Your God provide for both of you
over the course of many years
You would not speak so utterly proud
Instead with gratitude you'd be touched

If you only knew what it's like
to see your babies grow
and witness as others who (think) they know better than you
step in and take over the position
that your God assigned to you
and tell them things they didn't need to know
about you and the mistakes that you've made
and by doing so, they lead their loyalty away from you
when all you did was raise them the best that you knew
and brought them to the church that saved and rescued you
because you knew that the real Jesus could be found there
and that Jesus was the only safe place to go.

If you knew what it was like
To have their knowledge blinded teachers tell you
Your child's not a reader,
and you inspired by love fought for them
against their planned marginalization

Then have to hear their doctors tell you,
"They're failing to thrive. In fact, this other one's insane."

But Your God through a true man of God tells you the Truth
"My child, They won't need Ritalin any more.
A hospital's not the place for them.
Both are HEALED by the blood that I have shed."

Then not just one, but all of them thrive and grow up strong
How soon they forget, that it was you who brought them
To the foot of the cross when they were small.

If you knew how it felt, that -- by listening to others
Your mother, their sisters and their brothers and others
Who (think they) know so more than you
Your little ones now growing up go astray
and are drawn away by their know it all evil influence
If you understood that kind of pain, that level of agony
that a mother of an offender has to pay
If you felt what she felt too
When she did the best she could
To raise them in the right way
Yet, despite all of this
Her offspring made their own "informed" choice
to end a life, to smoke some dope,
to steal a car then run and hide
or even to rape a child

The pain that strikes her heart is brutal
But it was because of her God, that she did not die
Though the mother part within her grieved
in many ways, that mother hope within her fainted
Though yet alive, she carried within her

a heart that was full of shattered glass
As she had to let them go and let the Law take over her part
And teach them harder lessons than
even she could ever think of to disperse
all because they refused to learn from her
and from those she knew
who understood what was the best way to go
Instead she had no other choice but to let her little ones go
Because the Law had come in and had taken full control.
Do you know what that felt like the day that she heard?
What else could she do?
When her God prepared her for this very moment
so many years ago, what else should she do?
But throw her wounded soul upon her God
Because she knew her Lord
she committed her baby's soul unto a Sovereign God
in complete and utter trust
and stepped back to serve her God by His power
with tearful eyes fixed on HIM, her Savior-Lover,
Jesus Christ.

If you weren't there when God gave her a word
And you didn't hear the things she heard
Could you really say a word at all?
Do you not realize what you're saying now
sounds so absurd?
If you truly understood this,
you would not be so quick to judge
To speak so harshly 'bout the things you know nothing about
If you knew THIS, you too would be still and know
(As she has always known)

That Her God IS GOD,
And HER God is in FULL control.
Then and only then
Would you even be qualified to have an opinion
that might stand because you've walked with her
like her Jesus did, through it all
But then... if you really knew
Would you even want to say a word?
Instead, you'd take her hand
And with her fall before her God
Worshipping HIM in immense gratitude
Understanding this;

It could have just as easily been you.

****

Excerpt from "O Be Careful, Little Eyes"
(Kids Action Bible Song)

O be careful little heart whom you trust
O be careful little heart whom you trust
For the Father up above
He's looking down in love
So, be careful little heart whom you trust.

****

The Evil of Opened Eyes
(aka opin-i-ons)

It's funny, how the people who have had so much to say
about your life
The one's who think they know better than God
what you should be doing,
You know, those people?
When you really need to know what to do
To make better choices that will benefit you in truth
They are nowhere around.

Now…they won't stand up for you
when you're called on the carpet by Jesus
for not fulfilling your purpose
But they have so much to say
(Like elephants in a three-ring circus)
Sitting you in their cars as they're taking you home
lecturing you 'bout you the things they see about you
that are "wrong"
"sharing" with you what they think that you should do
Constantly telling you that
you need to DO Something… with your life
(after all, something is better than nothing, so they say.)

But what they don't know is that… you already were.
You were walking out on the waters of your purpose
You were walking by faith, and NOT by sight)

but just because they CAN'T see it,
they just won't leave you alone.
(Well... actually, they do)

When you fall on your face,
and your heart and body turns black and blue
When you're at a crossroads,
seriously needing to know what you should do
Somehow they grow silent, and walk right on by you
Because after they're done, they tell themselves that
You're someone else's problem now.

But what they don't know is that all of them together
Don't even have a clue
Not one of them was there,
when God, through your pastor spoke
His word of right-eous-ness... to YOU.

So when you're stuck in the middle
Of that path that you're on
That straggled path you took, instead of the straight one
All because of the lectures to you they gave,
Leaving you to have to clean up that mess that you made
Where are your "advisors" who spoke so profusely
To help you to sort it all out?
They are nowhere around
All that remains is you needing desperately
to make the RIGHT decision now
for the rest of your life
for once in your life.

You WERE on the right path
The one that was right for you
And now that you're out there, not knowing what to do
They're just standing by, looking
waiting to see if you'll fall
like you've done so many times before
All the while, while you're praying
"Lord Jesus, take my hand
Lead me back into Your promised land"
(how come when they ask if anyone has a prayer request
Not one of them ever steps forward to touch in agreement
regarding THAT prayer of faith …for you?)

So… How do you handle it?
When you want so bad to go to them and say
"How DARE you interfere
With the path I was on that was Graced?
With your shortsighted open eyes on
things you did not know nothing 'bout
how your meddling interference,
drummed repeatedly into my ears
and the stakes of your harsh assumptions 'bout me
driven so deeply into my heart
blocked the good that I was seeing
and obstructed the path that I was on.

I listened to you, (just to shut you up)
and none of you can tell me now,
what the heck should I do
Between all of your disdainful sentiments shared,
none of these was from The Truth

You had so much to say, back then
But you just could not see
past the thing I was walking through
that which only appeared bad,
but actually was God's GOOD
it was an affliction of the gospel that He knew
that I HAD to go through
Which if, I had remained
in the state and the place of His grace
all of it would have no doubt turned out for His glory
and for my ultimate good

But because you interfered
I've been thrown off my course
Were it not for God's intervention
My rails would have remain broken/
my life still all wrong
How I wish I could get back
To the place of MY grace
(I need not be jealous of yours)
And as for you, I wish you knew
that you were being used
As blind guides that I learned to listen to
Feeding me your Opinions, and not from the Word
of His Truth meant for me
How much you should know that I cannot trust you now
And no…you can't tell me anything else
But hello, how are you and good bye.
I need to get out of this ditch I fell in
For I refuse to remain in this erroneous position
While you've moved on

I want to go back into the place where I fit
The place of His grace and abundant provision
The place where I lived the best days of my life
Doing things I never knew I could
Working late hours when it felt like I worked only two
The place where I served Him in step with His Spirit
The place where I flowed
BEFORE you and your interference got into it
BEFORE I missed God by listening to you
and missed out on His best.

(And on those nights you took me home?
I should have just caught the bus.)

I want to be restored back into the place where work is rest
Sweatless victory, walking by the Word of the Lord
Reaping His rewards that were promised to me so long ago.
The more I hear about integrity, now, the more I realize
That I was walking in integrity all of the time
Until YOU, with your mouth opened up my eyes
To see things I did not even need to know
Now that I've seen them, what good did that do?
What now, can I show?
But a lot of undoing I have to rewind
For all the miss-takes I made. A lot of wasted time

All because I listened… A BLIND guide.

Am I talking about you?

I Miss My Child

I miss my child.
I miss his smile.
His voice. His song.
His laughter
His joking manner, even when it got on my nerves
I miss him
I miss his kindness
I miss the times that he doesn't want to do
what I ask him to
Pissing me off,
because I reaaaally needed to go to the store
And had to lug all those bags home in the snow
But then he manages to do something
so unexpectedly lovely
That I forget why I'm mad with him
In fact, I love him more.

I hate Facebook for being so available
For allowing our young people
to post whatever they want online
Luring them into posting things
that devastate their lives just because they could.

Or because some idiot friend told them to
And they, being so gullible, listened
And their life gets twist-turned-upside-down
In real time
In jail time

I dislike those who thought they knew so much
Enough to tell my son
Something that only his pastor, his father, or me could
have/should have told him
But instead, they butted in
Instead they just HAD to give
their 1/2 cent worth of advice to a child not their own
Advice that wasn't even worth the salt
that goes onto a cracker
But still, they just had to give it!
And told him what he was doing (in fulfilling his purpose)
just wasn't worth his time.
"You can do better than this!" that's what they said
And then, having listened,
my boy left the safety of the Will of God
for paths unknown, untried and untested
and now...
All because he left the path of purpose,
where he was safe
And walked in the counsel of those who were ungodly
Today, he's in a cell

Although to hear them tell it,
"they only meant him well."
My heart wants to scream!!!!!!!!!!!!!!!!!!!!!!
I want so bad to say to you:
How could you? How DARE you?
I would have never done that to your child.
But in spite of how I feel right now,
especially while writing this
I must forgive you and find my way clear

to release you in peace into the hands of our Father
So I can face you unaffectedly in true love.
Because that's something that I cannot pretend to have
And for me to hate you... is simply not worth my time to do
Because I've got my own purpose to fulfill
Just like you
And for me, even in this, it's worth it all
Besides, I know if I did confront you, it wouldn't do any good
You'd only deny it.
Because he's not YOUR CHILD.
So, as for me, what can I do but grieve in silence
Feeling like a bag full of broken, shattered glass
What do you care?
Your children are safe, they're not like mine.
As for my son.
My baby's gone.
He cannot speak to me, nor me to him
Except in prayer.

I see his picture in happier times
And know that now I just have to walk on through
Do my purpose despite everything I see,
Yet believe. And try to drive away the pain
that abides deep inside my soul that I feel.
I cannot just pick up the phone to call him
And he'll answer.
Not Anymore.
He can't just pop by, just to see how I'm doing.

No one... Anyone I call...
can't possibly understand what this is like for me
Unless you've been through it

And it's funny that most expect me to just be okay with this
And deny the experience I'm walking through
so they don't have to be bothered with the fallout of my pain
So to keep the peace, I keep my distance
Trusting my Lord every day over my emotions to reign
Gathering the courage to press on through
Because I know I must continue to do God's will
In spite of what I'm feeling
When, truth be told, if I told my truth
I'm not feeling this at all

But I go on
Staying busy, doing what I must...
Keeping the eyes of my heart FIXED on God
As I wait before my Advocate in anything but silent prayer
I know I need to be stronger than I am right now
(but honestly, I'm not)

But I'm supposed to just take it, Right?

Not cry.
Not be angry.
Not want to kick somebody's ass
Not scream deep and loud from the depths of my soul
and break (just about) everything I can
(except the things I can't replace)
But I can't.
In myself, #IAMJUSTNOTTHATSTRONG.

I wish I really could stop feeling
Turn off the screaming
Put out the fire
Untighten my stomach
Silence the roaring in my ears
Plug up the waterworks gushing forth from my eyes
And just be nestled safe in my Father's heart.
Because life, as I know it, must go on.

So pardon me if my humanity's showing
My niceness has left the building...
Because I miss my son
Ever longing for my baby.
MY baby. My child...
To be as he once was

Safe in the will of God.

Happy Mother's Day?

With all the Happy Mother's Day accolades
I hear all around me
on today, all I want to do is
to be wrapped in His embrace
For I don't feel at all like a mother
Though I have had children
I feel nothing like the warm and fuzzy motherly feelings
that I guess I should be feeling
On a day like this, I feel "otherly"
When I hear Happy Mother's Day
I feel like they are talking to someone else
And it doesn't really matter much to me.
For it does not apply to me.

I just want to be wrapped up
In the warmth of Love
Want to be caught up
In the splendor of Amazing Grace
Want to be tangled up
Hidden in The Everlasting Arms
Where the wicked cease from troubling
where I can be renewed and start again
I'm not sorry
For what I did is done
I won't apologize
For the road that I walked
At the time, I had no other choice
And I will not grieve anymore
Can't feel the pain anymore
I'm not mad anymore
For I forgive
The anger is gone
The fighting is over

I've given it all over to God

No dinners. No presents. No kisses do I look for
because I know for that I didn't sow
I just want to be wrapped up
In the warmth of His embrace
Want to be caught up
In the splendor of His Face
Want to be tangled up
Hidden inside His Heart
I want a brand new start

I cannot rest until the children that I bear
have the Love for Jesus In them
And a thirst like I do for You, Dear Lord
Right from the start

So wrap up all of the Mother's Day greetings
Wash them all away
I don't care anymore
If I am acknowledged
For I was only one, two, three times a mother by default

So save your Mother's Day accolades
For another day
Give your roses to another one
Who has worked at motherhood long and hard
And skillfully earned it because her children praise her
as for me, this is just another day
For I cannot bear to acknowledge something
That came before my time

Instead let my fertile ground be turned over
And washed out thoroughly by His Blood
Let my natal womb be prepared for something new
To receive a righteous seed
planted by One whose heart is True
and let bygones be bye-gone
for grieving over this I'm through

I can't cry anymore
I see you, but I can't feel for you
Can't feel you because you're not mine
And all I want to do
Is say good bye
And be wrapped up
In the warmth of His embrace
Want to be caught up
Blinded by the Brilliance of His Face
Want to be tangled up
Reachable only through His Word
with His love dominating deep in my heart

The life I had
I feel nothing for
all I long for now
Is a righteous tree from me
to come forth

A goodly heritage
Birthing those who will willingly bear the Love of my Jesus
Right from out of my heart
As they slip out of the Womb of my
Re-created Spirit

Into the Loving Hands of My God
Living their lives forever unto Him.

I long to start over all over again
And I will not rest…
"…till he establish, and till he make
Jerusalem (Crystal) a praise in the earth."

"Thou shalt no more be termed Forsaken; neither shall thy land anymore be termed Desolate: but thou shalt be called Hephzibah, and thy land Beulah: for the LORD delighteth in thee, and thy land shall be married. For [as] a young man marrieth a virgin, [so] shall thy sons marry thee: and [as] the bridegroom rejoiceth over the bride, [so] shall thy God rejoice over thee.

I have set watchmen upon thy walls, O Jerusalem, [which] shall never hold their peace day nor night: ye that make mention of the LORD, keep not silence, And give him no rest, till he establish, and till HE make Jerusalem (Crystal) a praise in the earth."

Isaiah 62:5-7 Amplified

Jesus is That Kind of Place

In life, things happen.
Things you think will happen, don't
people you fall in love with, don't return the love
They always choose another who is
prettier, taller, slimmer or less complicated than you
Leaving you to wonder, what the hell is wrong with you
when there is nothing really wrong with you at all
when children that you've hold out hope would change
and turn back to what they know is Truth
remain the same and then blame you
and people insist on asking you all about it
fix the eyes of your crushed up heart on Jesus

You take a step and fall,
in the pursuit of your call
computers pop, they turn off
and the people that you're serving, laugh
and under a rock you want to crawl
Crawl to Jesus

When the unexpected happens
right in front of everyone
you've got to keep on going
got to keep on moving on
No matter what it feels like
Jesus cares for you, that's all
that really matters in the end.
He will be your Bestest Friend
Better than the ones you think would understand
He understands you better in the end
that's all that matters

So fix your eyes
on the One who died to make you whole and know
the silent cries of your heart that you can tell to no one else
you can pour them all out on His
You can tell it all to Jesus
He's the One who Truly cares
Let Him be your shock absorber
when life hits you in the face, instead of crying tears of pity
Rejoice!
and then be filled with His amazing Grace
as you Fix your eyes on the Love in His face

Walk around at large anyway
even if you have to crawl after falling flat upon your face
His power will have you walking anyway
Learning that it's in your deepest weakness, that you will
discover His amazing strength
will never let you down
will keep you going
even when you think you can't go on
you must!
for you have a job for HIM to do
you'll discover in the end, that He really does get you
So keep on keeping on for
Jesus. And Yes, for His people too
For Jesus! Sweet Jesus is the one
Who really is that Kind of Resting Place
for you.

Note to my Younger Self

I finally know what I would say to my younger self…
I'd say,
Don't you listen to ANYTHING that the devil says to you
No matter how dark the night
If you hold on to the hope of God
Eventually Jesus will bring in His light to you to deliver you
And then He will take you on a journey
and make of you
A "Crystal-LIGHT" of his design
For Him to shine
His light through you

A forged heart has now become
a diadem in the hand of her God.

And then I heard the Holy Ghost within me say, *"You shall also be a crown of glory in the hand of the LORD, and a royal diadem in the hand of your God."*

I said to Him, Amen.

The Reintroduction to Me

There comes a time in one's life
Where enough must be enough.
I am tired of quitting and starting
over and over and over and over again.
I cannot put myself through another setback
(or could it be a set UP, this time?)

I have done without so much, for so long
All because I gave up way too soon
Instead of giving it my all for a long period of time.
How much more do I have to fall
Before I get the point that running away and falling
is NOT worth it after all.

I NEED to grow up
And manage the things that I should
The things that will take me to the level I've been longing to
see
So I can truly be trusted by God and by men to handle more.
Isn't it enough yet
I cannot do this any more.
I want to reap the things I've been longing for.
Six months of consistency and I can upgrade my car
A year to eighteen months more, who knows?
Maybe then, a house I can call MY own
In two years, a mate, perhaps?
Who knows what else is in store,
only God.
But I've got to get through this phase

In order to see it all unfold.

I hate the fact that the people I know
Don't want to see me make it.
They treat me like I am still the fool I once was
(and honestly, if it wasn't for God's intervention and
education, the one I still would be)
I am so fed up with their flakiness toward me pretending that
they care (yeah… right!)
And the people who "know" me, the ones that I love, don't
even see ME at all,
I'm tired of being anything other than the me that I am.
I LOVE that me that I am, now
I refuse to become something I'm not
Just so that I can fit in to a mold that I never did
So, I just need to let go… and move on

The people that "know" me,
Need a reintroduction
They need to step back and be educated
to the me that I am now
So that these people can get the point
that this disrespectful treatment toward the me that I
and my Heavenly Father know
Stops now. And I'm not "just kidding"

How on earth can we expect
to love those who are on the outside
When we are so condescending to
those who live and serve amongst us all the time?

I am not a little girl any more
And this is not South Shore High School
I'm not running away from school to school to school,
then from job, to job to job to job to job
and then from church to any other place
for there is no other place, than the place of His Grace
I'm not running anymore
Away from these grown ass bullies
The ones who are wrapped up in titles and status
The ones who think I am nothing more than what I was
When I first walked in the door
But…in Christ, I am complete
in Him and in who I am
you need to get that through your head.

I do not need your permission to be who I am
Just in case you did not know, just like you,
I have a RIGHT to be here!

So rather than fight in the only way I know how
(arguing with my voice)
I'll just step back, step away from you,
and let God handle this
And focus on my chosen course
Because, like you, I have a job to do
And I won't let you interfere, this time
The purpose I have is just as important
As those who refuse to acknowledge it

So, instead of debating the point, I'm done
I'll just say NO to your endless requests

And NO to the things
that do not serve my higher purpose.

You see, I am learning to reject the good and evil
In favor of that which is all good.
That which is truly the good of God

I Rise

I am not a quitter. Anymore.
I may have fallen
I may have failed
I might be broken
But I only look that way right now
Because as long as I have breath and I have the Spirit of God
Almighty within
I'll just get back up and do it again.
The decisions of my children
Are NOT mine.
Neither are the choices of my family of origin.
I have the right and now the responsibility
To make decisions and choices
That accurately reflect MY heart.

As Jabez prayed, LORD Save ME from this legacy
I pray to my Advocate to rescue me from what would be
Without His Purpose and His Grace on me
I refuse to accept that because my kids were fools
That I have to be.
That is NOT for me.
I'm in this to win, this time
To make the rest of my life
The best of my life, this time
For Jesus to be praised

To see the glory of the LORD show out on my behalf
And witness everything turn around for my good
In the midst of those who have seemingly lost hope

In themselves and yes, even in me
I will rise to glorify my Lord
Not by my own ability
Nor by my own ingenuity
But empowered by the Word of my life's mission
breathed into me
By God.

In Love

I wish I was in love
And looked into strong and silent eyes
Of one full of trustful love
For me.
Our hearts beat together in
Agreement to walk as one
In purpose, passion and grace
To serve together, hand to hand
Giving the best of ourselves
To the Lord and then to man
To each other in bountiful generousity,
we pour.
(sigh) I wish I was in love.
I wish I was in love
When my heart fell wide open
The one I loved
Caught it and held it
Gently within His own
The one whose heart I longed for
Truly wanted me in return

The man I loved
At last would be the one
with my life I could trust
whose leadership I could glean
his wisdom I could learn from
my life with Him enhanced
Because we both know it is not God's best for us
to remain alone

together, in agreement we'd fulfill His plan

(sigh…) How I wish I could be found by such a one
Who…makes my heart skip a beat
And my eyes glaze over
And my breath catch
Because he looked my way
(I can't go near him to this day…)
The words coming from his eyes
Told me all that he needed to say
And I heard him
(Because I have a feeling that if I did… he would know.)
I am so sorry I missed
Such a one.
Because of my misstep, He is gone.
But in spite of this, my life must go on
Although, I can't help one silent prayer…
Lord, could there be
another one?

For Real – The Prelude:

I am loving me the RIGHT way. first, I am treating myself the way that I treat other people: with love, care, concern and true respect. I'm making better quality choices for my life and love expectations. Today, the decisions I make will be the tools that will bring out the best that's already within me in every area of my life. I don't want to be self-centered, because that is a prison of self-isolation. Instead, I want to be centered (the Bible calls it being rooted and grounded) in the Love of God, so that I love everyone, from my future husband to even my enemies from a stable place. That is what I choose to do today.

For Real

I am of Love, and my heart is huge.
Therefore, I cannot hide out in fear or dread of my life.
I am born to live and to live out
my life my heart in its fullness.

My feelings are mine
and I will not deny them.
As big as they are, I'll let them be
As strong as they come, I'll not let them rule me,
but I will feel them
and embrace them fully as a part of who I am.

I will not apologize
for the creation God has made me.
For I am of His design.
My Father loves me, in all my fullness
and I will trust Him, even though right now, all I feel is pain,
I know He will heal me, because He loves me.

So the love I show others will be from deep within me
The Love I am will be for real.

My compassion, expansive,
will be as wide as the sea.
the passion I have, directed positively
the drive deep within me to nurture and care
I'll disperse on the hungry, the lowly, the needy
and not to the greedy, who do not receive me
the gift that I am will not go to waste
for I love who I love
and I cannot hold it back
for I am meant to be free
I am love. I am loved,
and I'll love who I will
as long as He supplies it
I'll be the one
who will see the need
and fill it
the Love I am and the love that I show
will be for real.

and you will know it.

The Truth of Imperfection

I am not perfect.
So stop expecting me not to make a mistake
Stop beating me up when I fall
Stop pounding on me with your expectations
And let me breathe
To rise once more

I am not without flaw
I react in ways I don't always understand
I run when I know I should stand
I want to stop but most times I don't
Even I wish I could understood why
The mask of perfection I've been wearing
All these years
Is now crumbling to dust in my hands
And now you see the real me
I'm all I have left
Can you love me?
Knowing full well who I am

Manipulate you
For what?
It's never worked before
It takes way too much to please you
I don't even want to try to anymore

Do you care?
Can you hear?
Not the sound of a pitiful woe is me

But the cry deep within my soul
Saying I've simply had enough?
All these years of trying to please you
Never worked
All my talent laid bare before God
And now you see the real me
I'm all I have left

Can you love me?
Knowing full well who I am

I need Jesus
To be right
I need all that He is
To be pleasing in your sight
So until I can touch the helm of His garment
I don't care what you think of me anymore.

The Mask I Won't Wear

I cannot wear a mask
Pretending that all is honky dory when it's not
Do my job without you asking
"So, what's going on?"
As if you really cared
When you and I both know that you don't.
Your saying "I'm crazy" is just way too easy
Then to really want to understand the why behind the why
behind the why
If I told you, You won't believe me
Not everything is melodrama
Some things are really important to me
Every heart has its limit
And I'm at mine
I cannot wear the mask
And lie.

I cannot wear a mask
And smile before you
Telling you all
what you want to hear
When the truth of the matter is
I only want to leave
And move far away from
Here.
I know I need to do things right
Bring closure to the things I've started
I know I should but can I do it
Without having to give account of myself
to every look and gaze?
Every question that demands an answer,
must I give an explanation?
NO!

Can't you all just back away from me
And let me breathe
Perhaps then I can thrive
And walk in the way that GOD wants me to?
Without your "intervention"
Do you think that's doable?
Can I just come and hear a Word from MY God
Without you pushing me and shoving me
Assuming so much of me
Just take your hands off of me
And let the Wind of His Spirit blow over me, washing me
Bathing me
So I can stand up in the power of His might
and move forward
Without the imprints of your gossip, your assumptions, your
judgments all over my back

I cannot wear the mask you expect from me
I cannot answer in the way that you need me
To be anymore
Because right now, the thing that I NEED
Is to be in my Heavenly Father's face
And just be before Him
So I can absorb HIS Grace
So I can believe once again
In me
without your "help"

But you can't take what I'm saying right now for an answer
Because it's just too much honest for you
You assume that
You know me so well

Well, what you all think you know about me
can all be tossed over a hill

say what you want,
At this point I really don't care.
My heart is real bruised and I've had enough
My face won't fit this pretentious façade
The mask I must wear to be in your presence
And it hurts way too much to face you without any protection
But as long as I show up and do what you need me to do
You don't care.
But I do.
And I won't wear a mask
Just for you.
Anymore

Every heart has its limit
And I'm at mine
I will not wear a mask
For you.

Through the eyes of a child
on behalf of children and their parents

The foundation of a child's life is love. And acceptance.

To shake that foundation is cruel and unusual punishment to the heart of that child. We should teach our children that they are loved, accepted and forgiven no matter if they make us so mad that we want to whatever, Even if we have to chastise them, we should not punish them by **ostracizing** them, without at least turn around and teach them that we may need a minute, or they need to consider their ways; ESPECIALLY when they are little or very young. Whatever we do, we need to reassure them that that foundation of love, acceptance into our hearts and families, and forgiveness is still there for them. We should let them know that. I don't think we, as parents, realize the impact that we have on our children.

We chastise them without explaining why, we yell at them, drag them off of buses and out of cars, we cuss at them, (and then get mad when we hear them say the very words they've heard from us.) We squash their need to understand, belittle their feelings and little choices/decisions, punish them for asking questions and even when our little one say 'no' to us, we get offended and take it personally, instead of understanding their process of discovery, their process of learning and becoming autonomous. That process (guided, of course) is a journey that every child has a RIGHT and a need to go through and is critical for them to become a whole person who is able to love back, to trust and say yes to what is expected of them, willingly. That wholeness of character is birthed from a foundation of Love, acceptance and a sense of belonging that never changes that is rooted deep within the heart of children at a very young age. From that firm foundation comes the ability to trust, to explore and then... to grow up, to thrive and then... to bloom.

Now, on the flipside, there is a place for a time out. A separation, when needed. But never as a means to control, shame or degrade, nor as an outlet to express YOUR own anger issues. But to table things as a means to regain a proper perspective (on both sides) and to allow for age appropriate consequences to play themselves out in the life of that child. Anything outside of this is an injury that has deep and lasting ramifications in the foundation of that child's core security. (How cruel is that?) Which forms cracks in that foundation to where they are shaky in every relationship they enter into. How can they learn to trust anyone (even God) that way? Then they have to go to school and experience interactions with others that have gone through the same? And we wonder why children today do what they do online and on the streets.

Parents, NEVER shake that foundation. Represent God's love rightly. Set your children up for success in life by loving them unconditionally.

For Mom. (On Mother's Day)

Time. and God.
Heals all hurt (if you let it go and let God have it.)
I miss you, mom.
I miss what we could have had.
what I wish we would have had, if only you had believed
my heart pours out the last of the grief
I've refused to feel
because life with you was so painful
but I am grateful that you were MY mother
because sometimes, tough meat needs to be tenderized
so that when it's tasted, it's tender and pleasurable in every bite.
I get that.
(Remember The Strong Willed Child, by James Dobson?)
I'm not mad at you, you did what you knew
I just miss you

Happy Birthday, Merry Christmas. Happy Mother's Day
Thank you for every gift you gave me.
your life, your sense of style and make up
your singing to Nancy Wilson records
your singing the Mamas & The Papas
to me when I was little
your insatiable thirst for understanding, leading you to read
and continually educate yourself
to where I had the best library in the world,
right there in my living room
even about things I did not need to know at the time
but because you were a nurse, I still had access to.

I miss the best of you.
but I do not miss the worst you were
I did not deserve that... at all.
but I forgive you
I understand that you did not know what else to do
I'm sorry that I never understood who you were
and why you felt the way you did at that time.
You've fought the whole world off, but could not see
it was never your battle to fight.
I understand that now.
I just wish somehow you could realized
just how much you were loved, just as you were
maybe you'd still be here.
but I understand you felt you needed to leave
and so, you just let go
and let us all go too.

I miss you.
but I get it now.
I understand. And it's okay.
the little twitch of pain i felt
was grief leaving my heart
as I release the last of you to God

This year is my year to celebrate
The woman I am now.

Let Go

You can't run away from yourself
You can't hide out from that thing in you
That only He can rout out
Being angry makes no sense
When God is God and you are not.

Holding it inside only hurts you the most
It is whatever it is
Why not just trust your God
To work things out
Why not just trust your God
agree with Him
To walk you out

Sometimes you can't help the hand you're dealt
Even if you did it to yourself
Won't help you to fuss
and crying 'bout it's not the way.
When you've done all you know to do
Running from it's not the thing you need to do
Might as well let go
And let God lead you through
You'll find that Jesus
is a Friend that sticketh closer to you than even a mother

You'll find that He is Everything you'll ever need
When you believed that you received
It's cause you've agreed that it is for you
And talking it over with Jesus

Makes the stormiest sea be peacefully still
And turns your darkest night bright
At the command of your word

So when you can't help the hand you've been dealt
Even if you did it to yourself
And the corner you're now in
Has no way for you to win
Won't help you to fuss
and crying 'bout it's not the way.
You can't run away anymore
Because there's nowhere to get away
From yourself

So You might as well let go
And let God take full control
At the sound of your cry
At the command of your word
You'll find Him faithful

Let Go
Of how you think you should come out
Let go
Of what you think your God should do
To work things out

What does it matter
as long as you know
He's been faithful,
can be trusted to make a way
through the fire, through the
flood
into a wealthy place
just for you
So just hand it over to the Lord
And keep his way because you do
know this...
That you are His

You can let it go
and let your Father have His way.

Love's Honesty

I never thought I would ever want to
Give you more than you're worth
Just so you'll look sheepish and silly
When I hand you over in cash
what you think I wouldn't
Giving me that fake ass smile
Telling me you love me with the Love of my Jesus
When I know that that's a lie
But what good would that do
When I know that it is I who need
To truly love you more
For that I thank you
For your narrow minded view of me
Makes me need Him more
Until He, by His power transforms my view
To a wider angle lens
So I can capture His point of view
The sting of your opin-eye-on-me
Takes nothing away from Whose I am
Cause this is not about me, but you

It matters not what you say to me
nor how you choose to come to me
I am, I AM who God says I am:
A New creation! The Old Things ARE passed away
And ALL THINGS are NEW
Even if you insist on seeing
my old dead grave clothes and mistake them as
the me you think you know

oops, pardon my dust, as I keep on walk forward
into a lighter day, a brighter day, a perfect day
the fact of this still remains
a fact that you cannot take away: that I am a NEW Creation
and MY life is hid within His Heart

So, Father, Grace me with Your Love even the more
So that the response from my heart toward my Earthly judges
be full of true graciousness
No hitch of hidden bitterness or resentment
Can stop my get-a-long

But I'm Free and UNBOUND
from their narrow minded opinion of me
Even if they yet and still judge my future actions
on the basis of old things that exist no more.
And though my flesh really aches to tell them plainly: "Look,
you really need to take the mote out of your own eye, and get
a clue! before you point out the splinter in mine."
But even that... is not worthy of my time
I only write to vent out my pissed offness of their snide insults.
So the next time I see them, I won't cuss 'em out,
"--ill-sitch!" (sorry, Father... strike that.)
Instead I know the thing I am to do
I simply need to love them through You
Not to make them feel better
Not to prove they're right
Not to gain their approval, nor to say I'm sorry
('cause honestly, right now, I'm not)

Not to even prove anything to them

or to anyone else that I'm any different
Than the me they think they knew
But because my Savior loved me first
When I was a whole lot worse a wretch
than what they think I still am
someone you did not want to know
But Jesus did.
He stooped down to my lowest level
And lovingly gave me his Grace
He let me see the truth
the pureness of His love for me
The purity of His acceptance of me
Caressed my face with Light
Even in the sorry state I'm in
He reached down and took me in
And that is why I love Him so
And the need for me to love you
He demands of me to bestow
Even more.

So, I forgive you
And regardless of how you view me.
I will learn that you are beautiful
Created by God
A needed part of our body.
You are a part of me, and I of you
Even if, to you, I am unseemly.
To God, I am no less important.
Nor are you, my brother, my sister
I just want to see you be made whole
Amen.

Go Through

There is nobody who never goes through nothing.
But the point is to go on through.
As Jimmi Hendricks said,
"break on through to the other side"
(just not the other side he meant)
Jesus told those in the boat with him,
"Let us pass over unto the other side"
Knowing (as only He would)
that there was a storm ahead
He chose to fall asleep confident in His Father's care
His disciples may not have had a clue
They should have known what to do
But He knew
Just go on through\Go on through

There is nobody who hasn't had a broken heart
Someone whom you thought was the one
Changed his mind and then from your life departed
But the point is not to let the pieces lodge
With feelings shattered and crushed
You can still go on
Don't let this make you numb
Just fall into His Arms assured
there'll be another
Something better than the one that let you go
If you just hold on/hold on
To what you know is The Truth
And go on through
Go on through

Move past the point of present pain
The sting's still there but don't be shamed
Keep moving forward for the victory is yours
And go on through/break on through
For you there is more
If you can get to the other side
You'll smile instead of cry
Just go on through/go on through

There is somebody somewhere
That needs what you're going through
Someone who may not make it
If they don't meet up with you
So hold on to your faith
And don't give up the fight
Just go on through
By the power of your Saviour's might
There's somebody out there
Encouraged by what they've seen in you
Even though you feel discouraged
They see The Lord's hand on you
bringing you out of this mess you're in
into something new

So don't camp out
in the wilderness of a cloudy misperception
Take his hand and let Him lead the way
Into your wealthy place of satisfaction guaranteed
Just go on through

Through the storm

Through the rain
Through the rip in your heart
That makes you think you'll never be the same
Even though you know you should smile
But all you feel like doing is cry
go on through
go on through

You'll make it
(just go on
If you can take it
(just go on)
No need to fake it
(hold on)
Cause you're an overcomer
(and you can take it)
Greater is He
That is in you
Than that big old mountain
That's facing you

Go on through, Go on through it

The Lord's got your back
His name, He speaks in front of you
So don't you turn around now
No time to give up now
Keep on moving, Keep on moving
Keep on moving, Keep on moving
Until you reach the other side
Not in the sweet by and by

But in the nasty here and now
in the presence of your enemies
and the ones who saw you down and out
You'll have it better than before
He's doing a new thing in you
But you've got to make it through
Just go on through.

Closure -- The Right Way

This was written to my biological dad, who I have met, and out of respect, shall remain unidentified. Dedicated to all those, like me, missed out on a father presence growing up. Know that you have an unseen, yet ALL Powerful One watching over you, even now.

Dear Dad;

I know that this is a long message, but I thought about you this morning. And though it probably would not make any difference, I felt the need to write to you to try to communicate my thanks for you. I know it's a little long, but there's a lot on my heart I'd like to share. And I promise you I am not putting you on blast. I'm writing mainly out of curiosity, and to bring closure to a nagging thought I've had for a while. I know I'm not a child, I've crossed over the 50-yard line and am embarking on the second and to me, the best of my life on earth. I have you to thank for that. God allowed you to be my father. He approved of you to allow you to meet my mother (under whatever circumstances that might have been at the time) and allowed you two to hook up and (intentional or not) you both create me. I am here because of you. My mother is deceased. I cannot thank her for her part, or bless her for even trying to raise me as best she knew how. My grandmother is pretty much gone, too. I cannot bless and thank either one. All I have left by way of an earthly parentage to bestow any kind of honor (beside my pastor) is you.

I understand the times, what they were back then. I do not have any anger or animosity toward you. I do, however wonder what you think of me. Or if you ever have thought of me, wanted to know about me, and mostly how you could have stayed away knowing that I existed. I know that there are two sides to every story and that, given how women can be, the stories do not always favor men. Seems like you all get blamed for everything. I am not that naïve to think that there was only one side to it. I guess, I'm writing because I just want to know: how could you be content to remain out of my life, even now. I'm asking because a new year is on the horizon, and out of all the messages I have sent, the letters I've written, I have yet to ever receive a response back from you. To me, that is sad. I am here, dad. I do exist. I am not after your money, (like at this point, I could get it anyway. It IS a little late on that.) But I do want to communicate with you. To see how YOU are doing. To have a small interaction with you, and I could not help but to try. If for no less reason but to say thank you for allowing God to use you to bring me here so that I can do something special for Him.

There is a lot that I received from you. My creativity, my love and knack for the artistic. My intelligence. I look at your facebook page on occasion, and wonder what I've missed, and given that I have been richly blessed in my life, the only thing I could think of is that I never got to know you. Or even hear your side of the story. But I digress. If I never hear from you, I will not unfriend you (I admit that was a little childish).

I will just continue on as I have, and hope that out of all of this I've written, you know that there is a part of you out there who truly does love you and honors you for acknowledging (at least to me) that I did come out from your loins. And I mean no insult by that. May you find all the love and joy that you desire and God bless you for having me.

All my love,

Crystal

Is THIS Love?

Heavenly Father, I would like Your help on this one.
On something that I feeling so deep inside.
I need to know if this is from You above
Or if this is only Earthly puppy love.

I can't afford to make a mistake here
Nor ignore anything You want to say
I want to know -- Is it okay for me to fall in love?

This is oh so new for me
And I have none other than You to guide me through
I don't want to hurt or to be the one to cause the pain
I can't afford to waste my time
Years upon years only to discover he wasn't
This time, my Father I need to KNOW.

I cannot tuck and run away from this
For this is what I usually do
But this time, I know that I can
And must be free and open to love
For no matter what I face, I cannot be afraid
To feel for this man
(oh Father, how much he really needs You as His Father.
For he, like me, has been obscured)

I've got to keep a level head, here
And remain in Your hands the vessel that You can use
With YOUR lovingkindness

working through the Words I say
drawing him closer and closer to You
Other women, You have empowered to be
(I've read their examples)
an unmovable standard of YOUR unconditional acceptance
without compromise
and they did it, to their natural and eternal reward
and I really want to do the same, Father. For You.
So, I need to remain hidden within YOUR fearful and
amazing Grace
Yet be that hand of Jesus tugging this one
Captivating him by Your intoxicating and irresistible Grace
Joy unspeakable and full of Your glory dispensed into his life
pure and true
Saying to him without any conditions I set,
My son of My Son, you are truly Loved.

My heart's desire
I must sacrifice
So that this man, this gentle, yet worn out soul
Can come to You and be made whole.
I can't afford to be selfish here, Father
For my life is not my own
The outpour I feel toward this man is so strong
I cannot afford to misunderstand its intent
nor do I honestly want to misuse it
But I need to, by Your mighty Love and Power,
lay it all on the Altar
Of time and of Your Trust
Surrendering it over, so that You can temper the flow
This man, this soul deserves to know You

And be truly reconciled to our God.

Is this what LOVE is?
To let go of my life
My fear, is not.
My need to hide, all gone.

My desire for a husband of my own
simply cast to the side
Like Isaac on the Altar
And my deepest compassion, once hidden away for protection,
Now bursts forth like new wine free from the old wineskins
of hurt now forgotten
My love is so wide open
To become God's hook of salvation
toward such one I could love (is THIS Love?)

I do love this man, Father
But deep inside that which I feel is for his benefit
an ache to see him whole
This love I feel is honestly not my own.
Because before,
I could not feel this way
This is something different
That I did not expect to experience
I tried not to feel it
But it pushed out of the depths of me
Like a warming flood over me
And he was right there

So now the question becomes

The one I used to ask all the time
Can I this time be a friend
for Love?

Maybe this is Your anointing
For me to truly Love

Beloved, let us love one another: for love is of God; and every one that loveth is born of God, and knoweth God. He that loveth not knoweth not God; for God is love. In this was manifested the love of God toward us, because that God sent his only begotten Son into the world, that we might live through him. 1 John 4:7-9

No one has greater love [no one has shown stronger affection] than to lay down (give up) his own life for his friends. John 15:13 Amplified

A Letter to My Long-Lost Love

I love you.
Forever and always.
I will never not love you
Even if you never choose me.
Because you set a place at the table of my heart
That nothing can erase
You let me know that there IS a man who can follow
and have the back of another
Who preaches God's amazing grace
That makes me love you more

There will always be another
Taller, slimmer, prettier, better, brighter
More mature and less complicated than I
And you, as a man
Can have your pick of any and yes, you being the head, have
the right to choose someone other than I.
(The men I've known always do)
But in the eyes of my heart
Forever and always,
There will never be another you.
And if, by God's desire, there ever is, another one for me
You'll be an extremely hard act
For that one to have to follow
For in Christ, you were my first

You taught me that there really IS a man,
other than my pastor
Who loves God, and puts His purpose first

And that makes me believe in you
But unless Christ chooses to let you know
The feelings that are deeply stored
In truth, the things I see in you
You can simply call me Ms. Jenkins,
'cause from me, you'll never know
For I've learned that I cannot make you see
The blessings stored up in being with me
I cannot make you want to know
All the things I want to bestow
So I've committed you over to God.

For I have learned that real love cannot be forced,
and I'm tired of trying to fight
for something only God can do
(a woman getting up in my face over you
was quite enough for me, thank you)
I want no man other than the one God had in store for me
Even if that man is NOT you.

So because I missed out, I'll just have to let you go
and be the me that I am without you
And love you rightly - from a place of a sister
just the way you are; as a brother in the Gospel
this is the only way I choose to see you now.
Because I believe that the privilege of knowing you
Is better than not having known you at all

For you have shown me
that a good and decent man really DOES exist
A man who is not afraid to submit,

surrender and serve another man
That makes me trust you more
Because if you have God's back,
and the backs of those who serve His cause,
Then I know you'll protect and be a truly safe haven
for the right woman
(how I wish I were that one)
How I hate the fact that I've missed out on your love.
So I'll have to be content just knowing you
And appreciating the gifts that you bestow
And serve you only in ways
that will propel you forward
believing only the best for you
even if that best doesn't include…me
But I'll love you forever and forever more
More than you will ever know.

Why do I love so deeply?
Why do I love with my entire heart?
Why do I risk the deepest pain
And give out of the deepest storehouse of my heart?
Because I simply cannot help it.
For love is of God.

I try to stop it, I try to shut it up
But when I love, it always comes out full blast
Not considering who it's poured out on
Never thinking about the ramifications of loving someone
until it's done
And so, knowing this, I must pour it out into God
And commit my heart to my Savior to keep for me
For my love is like a thoroughbred

A stallion, full of passion and commitment
That needs to be channeled into the right receptacle:
My purpose and the people of God.

But in the recesses of my stallion heart
You abide forever, right up under Christ
Someone once told me that loving you
was only an infatuation, but NO!
Though over the years I've tried to forget you,
to stop what I feel and kill the hope of restoration.
I know now that I cannot
It's like the beating of my heart.
There will always be a place for you there
I... love... you.

Even beyond my lifetime, I do. Love you
with all of my human heart filled with the love of Christ
I do.
Love you.

Only you.

My National Boyfriend Day poem

I wish I could dismiss you from my eyes
It's so much easier to forget
If I can do so from a distance
Out of sight, out of mind
And eventually… out of heart
I really wish I could move
to a place far away where I didn't have to see you again
at least not in this life.

But because The Lord still has plans for me
I have to do so from wherever I am
Regardless of the things I see
I must learn to become blind
And in the midst of having to hear those who tell me
"No one wants to be with you"
Which hurts me deeply even when it's said in jest
I'm learned to say nothing and even laugh it off
Knowing deep inside that that simply can't be true
regardless of what it looks like
I'm learning not to care (at least in public)
whether or not they do
Because I know there is a Man who Loves me
and He's the only One Whose love's been true
This Man loves ME for who I AM
Even though He could never be a boyfriend
He IS my closest friend, tried and True
One Who never leaves me but sticketh closer
than ANY brother
He's the One who knows me better
Than my own mother

He took on the challenge of loving me
That the strong and the perfect in their integrity,
the smart and the seemingly mighty were

and honestly still are
Way too freakin' chicken to accept
He's the One Who knows how to reach me, inspire me
And motivate me better than most people that I know
Because this Man doesn't make physical, social, moral or financial perfection
A condition for me to have access to
His Amazing and Unfailing Love.
(Those perfections do come
But they come only through loving Him)

I'm blessed on National Boyfriend Day
To have the Bestest Friend
Who accepted, loves and cares for me
Paying the price for me to believe on Him
with His precious Blood
Which privileged me with a blissful security
By the powerful Words that He dispenses to me
And Through the purpose that He gave to me,
This Man enables me
to get up, keep going and keep on doing it
again and again
For Him.

The hope of His presence remains with me
and keeps me moving forward in confidence,
because He sees me beautiful
In spite of my cane, my weight
and the length of my naturally curly hair.

He speaks to me and moves me with His passion to reach an
unnecessarily lost and dying world
Because the World's already redeemed!)
In spite of the time that it takes for me (sometimes)
to get where I need to go.

But what He sees when He looks at me
speaks to me and fills me up
in spite of what I see around me
and in spite of those who can't see beyond my frailties to
behold the wonder of His Power within my soul)
He makes me His woman
His Holy Presence is my constant companion
And His love's what makes me whole.

So go your way and forget about me
Be happy with the things you want and know that I wish you well
I pray that you get your heart's desire
Cause Hating on you would not benefit me at all
And you're just not worth all of that.
Because I know that Jesus Loves me
and He's the only One
Whose love's been true

He loves ME for who I AM
Even though He'll never be a boyfriend
He IS my closest friend.
He makes the impossible, possible
'Cause HE did it Himself as a man
that's why I love and honor HIM
He IS to me and will forever be
The Almighty, the Great I AM!

Let me tell you about A Woman of God

This is written in honor of the women of God in my life who have imparted so much into me and have labored over me in prayer, some of whose names are mentioned here...
Mother Juanita Singleton,
Dr. Mary Ellen Strong, Annabelle Gaines Dye,
Diane Singleton, Pastor Linda Jackson
Marsha Herring, Julia Blakely
Magnolia Townsend, Frances Cornell
Sister Claudie Flynn, LaToya Butler
Jacqueline Miller, Clorene Roddy
Anita Cornelius, Sherlydine Dixon
LaShawn Givens
And my birth mother: Caroline Dye-Williams
This is my way of saying thank you.

Today I am so grateful.
My heart is so full.
I am living my life as a woman of God.
And now I can tell you why.

Women of God are not pansies.
Nor are they brash and loud.
They don't get all up in man's face,
except to smear it with prayer, kisses and love.

They don't demand respect, they command it
with the gentle way they walk and the sweetest way they call
you "baby"

just before they set you straight, in Jesus' Name.

They labor hard, but you don't always see it.
They feel deeply and love you fully till the last drop,
but most times you don't perceive it as you should
until after they've gone.

But when they've left, you know your life's been changed
forever and it's always for the better.

Women of God are the most unappreciated,
unrecognized treasure that we have.
Yet, they are the most needed.
A man just could not be the man he needs to be
without the right one by his side
or who rocked their cradle.
Women of God teach their children
how to rule the world
and not the other way around.

Women of God are the original "Ride or Die" chicks,
but they do it all for the glory of their Heavenly Father
and the love of a good man.
But not just any man. Their good man.

Women of God take care of business
with such class and finesse, they can handle it all
and take all they need to take
and still look like they never broke one nail,
lost one hair out of place, nor lost one moment of sleep.
If they're tired, hungry or hurt, you'll never know it.

Oh but don't you be fooled, they've often burned the
midnight oil before their Father
laboring over you in prayer,
as you walked out of that near death experience
shaking your head and wondering,
"Wow! How DID I get out of that?"

Women of God writhing in deep intercession
were the reason why that other person got that bad batch of
dope and lost their mind forever,
while you instead took a simple hit of a "clean" joint
and lived to tell about it to this day.

Women of God are as tough as nails
and they'll stick you with one if you mess with them, quick.
And their love for their men, their fathers, their husbands,
their sons and their pastors is like none other, because it's of
God,
their support for you is firm and fixed.
You can rest assured that a woman of God…
she's got your back because God, their Father has hers.

So If you are alive. If you're successful. If your needs are met
and your bills somehow get paid,
If today, you are walking around
healthy and whole in spite of the mess you've made
You'd better turn around and remember…
it's because of the laboring intercession of

a mighty woman of God.

Sittin' -- Reflections as I Unwind

As I write, I gain Clarity.
Putting pen to paper and touch my fingers to keyboard
pouring out my soul unto My Lord
my Heavenly Father's catharsis to liberate me
so that I can bless His World.

Sittin' in my favorite place
Sippin' on coffee as I watched
the raindrops on the window
Such a pretty scene.
Got rained on as I came here
And I didn't mind
Felt so good after scorching summer heat has plagued my
body for days
The rain calmed me down
And refreshed the cells in my skin
As I swear I heard them say ahhhhhhh
"Thank You very much for that."
As I sit near several women, blessed and wealthy, chatting
away
Appearing to enjoy each other's company
Not knowing the diamond that they sit beside
But... that's okay too.
'cause that is not where my mind is...

I reflect
As I look up and see the sky again is blue

I am unwinding
Unfolding and unbending
From the pressures of this season
And so, I smile
As I take my moment
To unwind.

This is been a week, I sigh
As I sit, I feel parts of me just release the tension
The anger and grief
As I unwind
I feel the muscles in my body release the tension
And go back to a relaxed state
And yes, I want to cry
I want to lay out on the floor and sleep right here
Or near here
Put my feet up and chill in the air
I wonder with all my heart, Oh Lord
HOW did I end up Here? In the midst of THIS?

A man has died and left this earth as mean as he was when I first met him
Even in his ending he still slighted
the people who truly cared for him
Living for nothing but himself
From his deathbed still controlling
Those who dared to minister to him
And if I am honest, when I heard that he left
I must admit that I was... HAPPY
And relieved that His tyranny of hate and negativity
was finally over.

And from that moment I began to unwind
And that is sad (I think.)

With each passing, I reflect
The message, the legacy they have left
And the funny thing is, I cannot be sad.
I haven't felt that emotion in a long long time
Instead I reflect on the messages I get
From the recalling of each life during the funeral
And reflect on how I want my own to be
Out of this one, I know what I DO NOT want
The bitterness , the pain and the grief

I had no idea that I could carve out my life
The way I wanted to
I thought life just happened
and you deal with whatever you get
But I know now that the opposite is true.
And now that I know that
I so badly want to develop my life
into something GOOD.
I've seen people leave here, and rejoiced
because I knew they had made it home
They graduated and the angels rejoiced at their arrival
On Earth their lives made everybody better
And I smiled because I KNEW that they HAD won

And I've seen people die
in varying levels of bitterness and evil
Causing pain as they made their exit
And at the end
Nobody really cared that they were gone

Even though they went on through the motions
Because it was the "proper thing" to do
But deep inside instead they all breathed a sigh of relief
Because their ministry was through.

Both ends of the spectrum of life were felt
And I alone am left to stop and reflect
As I write and unwind
I reflect

I almost ruined a really good person's help this week
Because of the way I said... what I said
And it scared me, and the lesson became very clear
Some people just don't take that shit
And I know that I'd better not ever do that again
Because I really do not want to be left all alone.
(to you, I am so very sorry)

Father God, I had no idea that I could choose
the quality and extent of my life
The way I truly want it to be
I thought life just happened
and you took whatever you get
I had no expectations
But I know now that the opposite is true.
That it is my responsibility to treat people BETTER than the
way I would want to be treated
In fact, how I am treated by others doesn't really matter
Because God promised that He would turn it all around
for my good.

And I am unwinding...
Reflecting and letting the tears of sadness flow
And I am unwinding
Taking moments that I NEED
To write and to reflect
as I sit and strive to bring to completion
the work set before me
I just needed this minute
As I am unwinding
Praying to my Father for Wisdom and direction
Clear information straight from His throne
specifically for ME
To make the RIGHT decisions this time
And I am unwinding
My chest is expanding
My stomach is releasing the knots it was holding in
For months
Settling down to it's peaceful place as deep inside internal
screams are released
As I write
Sittin' in my most favorite place
Looking out at beauty,
crying out for His glory
As I am unwinding.
Longing for my place in His world
A place in the heart of my family from heaven
A place where I truly belong

I unwind
As I realize I'd better get this work done
My mind becomes focused
And my life today has begun

I close the door on this chapter once again
Knowing that my Father God has indeed heard my prayer.
And I unwind, refuel, refresh
And begin this day again.
Amen

I now am calm.

Twenty-One (...Again)

Here I am
Arriving at maturity.
My whole life (anew) ahead of me
No longer trapped in what coulda-woulda-shoulda-been
I've been given a new opportunity
To live out my life for eternity.

I breathe in the breath of Heaven
Alive and vibrant it smells
I stand on the threshold of giving God His glory
My heart stands all aglow.
My face shines with his brilliance
My heart burns bright with His living Hope
(He gave me back my life...)
So now it's up to me to choose.

The life I live from henceforth
For Him or for the world.
But I've been there, done that
(and I have the scars to prove it)
My heart yearns for something better
Bigger, brighter
Living my life tighter, wiser, I'm a survivor
can't you see?
At TWENTY-ONE... Again.

Didn't matter what my birth certificate said
I am what God says I am

My youth is renewed like the Eagle's is
My life has only just begun
So I arrive at a place of awareness
My purpose rising like the dawning of the Sun
And I have a lot of living to do
A lot of ground to cover.

Maturity, responsibility
Living free
Peacefully
Defining my life by the rules of His Word
Walking by faith, in the same steps of Abraham
bowing deeply, humbly before my God when He appears
In full surrender, I do run without weariness
And I walk, refusing to faint
I yield my life over to His Supernatural Empowerment
And be filled to the overflow with his Spirit
Drinking deeply of His Love
It's no more I who live
But it is the Christ within
Living loud and strong through me
At Twenty-One… Again.

The Way Of Love

With each passing of time
There is an increasing responsibility
For the creation borne of purpose
To rise to the occasion, put away the childish
And embrace the way of love
The way of love.

Now is the time
To no more remember the offenses
That we caused each other
Time to put it all away
Cover it under His Blood
For His Grace is the only thing
That ties us together
Bound together forever
Under the Banner of His Love

The pain of letting go we feel
In time, will pass on by and joy will remain
As we show love one for another
For we hold a promise that will never die
Signed, Sealed and Ratified in the way of love
The way of Love.
Laying down our lives the one for the other.

No more time for religiousity
Petty bickering and the way of strife
Should no more be
For with each passing

Like the ticking of a clock
Comes the demand for us to live on, live on!
And to care for each other
Authentically
For that is the way of Love
the only way of Love

For by this, said Jesus, shall all men know
That you are of Me,
Is that you have My Love toward each other

So, my sister, my brother take courage
And hold fast to The Word of our Lord
That those who sleep in Christ shall rise
Because He lives, they do NOT die
we have a sure hope
they are with Him beyond the sky

So while we remain in the realm of time
we are to live as though it is Now
For our redemption is as sure
As the dawning of the sun
For that is the way of His Love
That IS the Way of Love.

Dear Father, i hurt. and i hate hurting all the time. being
needy as i have been.
and if i've ever needed anyone,
i need you now.

My Father's Thoughts to me

Would you be angry at a blind man/woman
who could not see?
Or a deaf person
because they COULD not hear you
when you speak?
would you be hurt at the dead
because they could not feel your pain?
or respond to your need?

Then why do you remain angry at
your mother, because she did the same?

My Close-Out Customer Service Policy from 1960 to Now

Let me explain my Closeout Customer Service policy:

- If I owe you money -- give me time. Either I WILL pay you, or God will compensate you for services you have rendered to me.

- If I did something to you, that was bad -- Please forgive me. If I knew better at the time, or understood who I really was and Who I belonged to, I would have valued you more and made a different and better decision.

- If I didn't do something I should have -- Again, forgive me. if I could have done it, I would have, and if I didn't, sorry. Maybe it wasn't the way that God wanted me to do it.

- If you expected something from me that I failed to do and thereby disappointed you in -- hasn't everyone? Guess that makes me human and a certain qualified candidate for His Grace, right?

If none of the above fits your case with me, please do not bring your complaints to me. Rather, refer all of your outstanding complaints to my Higher Authority in the Legal Department Who is over my Case-- Jesus the Christ, my Advocate.

It is He Who will empower me to address your situation on a case-by-case basis at the appointed time of His choosing. Who knows? Maybe by the time He gets to you, you will have already been compensated much better than I ever could.

This concludes my Customer Service Policy for all aughts and grievances of the past 49+ years of my time on earth and completes the close out portion of the first half century of my life.

Grace & Peace to you!

Crystal Marie Dye- Gaines
December 28

On the Night Before New Year's....

This is New Year's Eve
And I do not want to feel like this tonight.
I really want this coming year to be different.
I really truly do.

I am tired, Lord
Of being tired
I don't want to fight to be who YOU say I am
I just want to BE it
I do not feel like fighting
So I stay to myself
I feel angry
And I don't want to feel like this

Should I really care what other people think about me
I really don't anymore
I don't want to feel their disapproval
I want to live my life on God's terms alone
I just don't care anymore.
So I am here, Lord
To do my job
And I really wish I was someone else
So that people I'm around
wouldn't "know" me so well anymore.
I'm trying, Father
To turn off my feelings
To numb out my heart
So that I won't cry

But all I feel inside is helpless
And pissed off because I am
I am an adult now
And I have the RIGHT to be who I am
I don't feel like praying right now
Because I want a real answer.

Help me dear Lord
Because I feel like I'm sinking
On the night before a New Year Begins.

My Closeout List of Gratitude

My Closeout Thank you list of Gratitude begins with The Lord Jesus and my MOG: I thank you for all that You have brought me out of, brought me through, taught me, and most of all, put up with me as I learned and re-learned and re-learned and re-learned again. I appreciate you more than I can say. I am beginning the best half of the first century of my life because of You!

I appreciate the haters in my life because y'all drive me to seek the face of my God more and more. You cause me to depend upon Him for my validation and He has never let me down. I thank you for remembering the mistakes I made/make and bringing them up to my face. and that you think and don't mind telling me and others that I am unqualified to do this or that and that you think that God can never use me because I am so jakked up. and especially I appreciate and thank the ones who tell me that they wonder who in the world would ever marry me. THANK YOU! THANK YOU! and again I say THANK YOU! Because all of you give me the fuel I need to cling to my Lord Jesus Christ, and by His power to never give up nor cave in, because I KNOW BETTER. and when the Lord get finished with me, so will you.
But it doesn't matter to me either way, as long as God receives ALL of it for His Glory.

I am grateful for the fellows who did me the favor of pushing me away and rejecting me as your romantic interest. I thank and appreciate you. Because honestly, I wasn't ready for a relationship with you and would not have been the best for you at that time in your life. I harbor no hard feelings toward you, and its okay that you don't want me because I have lived a better life without you and have learned the tough lesson that I am worthy of love without you. My life did not end because you weren't there. In fact, I found out that I was and am worth much more than I realized at that time, and that I needed to find that out for myself. Who knows, maybe I never would have if you stayed and became my everything. So I am glad that you didn't. I am free and more of a woman now than I would have been had I been with you. You blessed my life, even though I didn't see it at the time. You made me a better, more mature woman for the one picked out for me by God. for that, I thank you and I ask God to richly bless you. (and don't worry, your names shall remain nameless, but if this hits you, well... It didn't mean to miss you. Its just not worth it for me to dredge up old diamonds. I love you anyway, Smooches)

Now, for those who stuck it out with me, I love you. Thank you for riding this life with me. for holding me and seeing me through the eyes of God instead of what even I could see. Thank you for your impartations. Your Words of wisdom. Your ears that bore my tears and screams that birthed new clarity and understanding of my life and journey. I love you and am excited about where God is taking me. To me, you are those rare individuals who chose to allow God to have his way in being His tool of perfection in my life.

For that I am grateful. (and don't worry, your names too shall remain nameless, but if this hits you, well... It didn't mean to miss you, cause I want to protect your blessing that you have coming directly from Heaven!)

For the rest, my new friends. HOLLAH! Let the best 1/2 of my first century BEGIN! WOO-HOO! At the landing strip of this New Year, I now: Know who I am, Love who I am, Know what my purpose in Life is, and am doing it. Can speak from a greater level of experience. More open to learning because I also understand that it's okay NOT to know everything. and I gratefully don't have the baggage of bad marriages nor angry babies daddies (because they were involved in their kids lives and helped them grow up suprisingly well to which I am grateful. AND I'm sane after having gone through a 1/2 century of drama and self-made issues) overall, I would say I'm blessed. And The BEST For me is HERE!

Happy New Year!

A Tree Just for Me

I went walking today
And it felt good.
Sat by a place just to talk with my God
To pour out my heart upon Him

I finished my walk and sat by this tree
Looking way up to the sky
And God directed my gaze to notice one tiny fruit on its branches.
I looked at that fruit wondering if that was an apple or a cherry
And what kind of tree it came from, never seen it before
So tiny, but perfectly formed was that fruit.
Then I looked up and around
And all around the branches on that tree
Were clusters and clusters of that same tiny fruit
And I heard His voice tell me   *"So shall your fruit be."*

And the more that I gazed into the branches of that tree
I saw more and more and more little clusters of that same fruit on that tree
Then I got up and looked at the tree
The sun shone brightly
Kissed warmly me on my cheek
Caressed my hand
And the Voice said calmly   *"and YOU are that tree."*

So I got up and I looked at that tree

And I saw that though it was short, it was very old
It had scars and lots of places where the bark had blended in
with the innermost wood
In places where maybe lightning had struck it and the tree
had survived and recovered
It had grooves, cracks and crevices and places where
The big branches were severed
It was twisted in places
But the tree as a whole was still there.
It had a place you could climb up and sit, like kids used to
when I was a child
Where the branches were grown as two
A boy could carve his name in one of the branches along with
his girl
In hopes that that childhood love would still be true when
they were grown.
(and oh how I wished I had a knife
or at least a Sharpie to write, CG and …who? You?)
But I digress
'cause all I talked to God about, was you.

I poured out my heart and the pain that was there
Of years that had passed
And the old wounds now laid bare
I cried and I cried because of the lovers I knew
Who did not choose to pick me, I felt like such a fool
And I wept before Him, laying my heart on Holy ground
as I dared asked Him – "Why?"

But the sun shone bright as I felt His caress
I heard Him say to me sweetly   *"but **I** picked you"*

So I gave it all over to God as best I could
And sealed my hearts cries with a kiss and a very long prayer
I cried and I cried as I put in my requests
For MY king. For me to be a Queen to the right one,
Not just to anyone
But a treasure for the one who from his heart
Would come and seek ME out
for I will only be found nestled within my Father's Arms

I then felt a peace from within
Knowing with all assurance
that He, my God had heard my prayer
I prayed for you
That He would take care of you for me
And give you a kiss from my heart.
I then stood up and gave over to Him
My Life, My love's loss, and My will.

Then I looked again at that tree
And the Lord let me see that the scars and the wounds and
the twisted and broken places and the intricate things I
observed
that up close appeared ugly
Actually made that tree what it was
Strong and sturdy
Hardy against the storms of life
It was the story of that tree
That tree will be around a really long time
Unmovable, not easily uprooted
A huge blessing to others.

Ants have their home within the wound of a broken place

And Birds helped themselves to the fruit of its branches
And not very many branches I saw
Did not have something on it
But clusters and clusters of ripening fruit I see everywhere
And the more I looked up
The more fruit that I saw
And I, again heard that Voice say
"Your fruit, the offspring of YOUR life will be like that, without number."

Then I felt the Sun touch my hand so gently,
tenderly saying to me
"Just hold on."

So I got up
Breathed out a cleansing breath of release
As I walked back home
My heart had a slight smile
Even though I was still a little sore inside
I was so ever grateful that I could talk to Him
For He hears me… And He loves me
And He really does take care of His own.
Amen.

Expression in Spanish...

Por Tu'

Te amo.
Por lo tanto te libero al amor.
Porque yo sé que en el amor, usted estarábien cuidada.
Si se trata de Amor que nos reunimos,
esta vez será más dulce porque el amor sin tiempo,
así que habrá experimentado.

Crystalle

My perspective on Why did I Get Married, Too"

A woman meets a man
and they
Create a marriage
A life together
But by what plan

Woman,
As your sister, I got to ask you
what do you want from this man?
You say the nicest things, you smile as you take his hand
But how do you treat his heart?
The trust he gives you, do you rip it apart
With your words? The high pitch in your voice?
Instead of being the virtuous woman using your strengths
to make him known among the elders at the gate
Do you use your hidden wisdom
To protect yourself and undermine his manly Grace?

Why? I ask Why DID you get married, too?
-- To have sex at your convenience
-- To have a convenient thrill
-- To do your thing and have a backup plan
-- using the man you say that you love
who must live with you and bear all your fallout, too?

(y'all don't here me...)

What hope then is there for those of us

Who still dream of that special love.

Women! Women!
Wake up! Wise up! Before it is too late
Oprah is NOT the authority
Of that love that only God can give you by His Amazing Grace.
(and OHHHH how do we treat our Master,
if this is the way we treat our men)

Stop listening to those who
Ain't got a man
Had a man they ain't got ovah
Bitter pills they peddle and want you to swallow
So you will vomit up the good man in your life
(Then you cry and complain that there aint no good men in this world)
I guess there wouldn't be
after dealin' with our mess, Lordee!

Silly women, who won't listen to God or their pastor
ain't got no business teachin No-Bod-Dee!
Its a woman seeking to be wise
who will run far and fast away from them
ain't been through nothin'
can't take nothin' off that man
(so they tell me, with a strong neck roll)
They can't tell you nothin'
'cause what in Hell do they really kno'?

After seeing "Why Did I get Married, too…"
All I really want to do

Is tighten up my relationship with God!
('cause I know that I can't treat any man really right,
if I've done my God, the One who gave His life up for me,
all wrong...)

(know what I'm sayin'??)

About Friendship

What is the purpose of your friendship? Have you ever asked someone "Why are you my friend? Or why do you want to be my friend? You should. Friendship, like a romance, is a deeply intimate connection. Not like sex, but close enough to merit either discovering or defining the purpose or end goal of connecting with someone. There should be an end goal in mind. Otherwise, how do you know if you and your friend are on the same pathway? If one or both or all of you doesn't step back and assess the nature of the friendships that you have and are cultivating, then what you're getting is what you want. Even if it's demeaning, negative, gossip-ridden or destructive to one or all involved. At best, it's dysfunctional if you haven't defined what the function of your friend-ship is supposed to be. What is the purpose of the support systems you have now? What are they actually supporting? Does it work beneficially for both of you? For any of you? If not, you really need to get a friendship checkup and not on Facebook.

About Love & Truth

I love you
And I care about you.
From you, and by you, I have learned a lot tonight.
From you, I have learned that if you really love someone,
Should you not provide a solution to them,
if you need to bring a fault to their attention?
In telling one the truth
What is love, if it is not first kind?
Should you not cover their error with the blanket of intercession
And then in active love, invest yourself in them
Lay down YOUR life for them
With the things they require
for them to make that change?

If you're going to criticize the way they smell,
Should you not provide the soap they need to clean, in a way that shows that you truly care?
How about being there to help them where they need it
And not just tell them what "someone said" about them
Is this what it means to speak the truth in love?

And by you, I have learned
that when one brings something to your attention
Are they sharing with you, their wisdom?
Or dispensing into you their fear?
In walking by faith, is there a balance between what man calls common sense and simple trust in God

Not considering the things around you,
just walking out on what HE said?
Don't you know that we serve an Almighty God?
How then can we be afraid, without insulting Him?
Should it not be a free and fearless walk by faith fueled
aflame in perfect Love (Which has no fear)
We can approach the throne of Grace in all outspokenness
Be not afraid of the pestilence by night,
nor for the arrow that flies by day
Is that not in the written in the Word that we trust?
Then why cannot we walk by this
when we do what The Lord says that we must?
Because the Word states
that perfect love casts out all fear
Or should we be considering the natural, normal things?
After all, they do exist around us.   NO!

In caring about me, be very careful that you do not spread the
"germs" of fear and apprehension
that you carry
Infecting me with apprehension in my forward actions once
motivated by the Word of Faith
Be careful that you don't influence movements
based upon what YOU see,
and not what God has said -- specifically to me
In giving me your advice,
be led of God and not of your carnal self-perspective
For if I listen to you, in the end, it is I who have to walk out
the fallout of what you've spoken
And if what you're telling me is not from God, and I stumble
from the walk of faith that I have come to know

Will you be there to walk with me through the darkness
Will your hand be there to help me back to the faith that GOD
has ordained for me to walk in?
No matter how well intentioned you might be in your advice,
Most likely you will not.
Because It's between my Father, the Word and I
Remember that Faith comes by hearing
and hearing by the Word of His Grace
And that persuasion comes from the top, down
and not from either side

Walking by Faith, in the light of His Face
That's the place I want to remain
So be silent in your speech if you cannot speak in support of
my trust in God
and speak that which will strengthen me in faith.

So why do you not consider the impact
of the words you speak
Before you speak them?

I love you, but I cannot receive the things you say,
if they're spoken out of your fear
I care for you, but I cannot absorb your voice
If it comes from the apprehension of
the things that cause you fear
I cannot allow them in my space,
I want to live in the place of His Grace
I no longer want to stumble in my walk
because of what you've said
I have to walk by faith and not by how things appear

Nor can I live by what you tell me
'bout what "someone said" about me
I don't care.
So please don't bring these things to my ears.

The only voice I want to hear
For the balance of my days
Is the one who brings to me
The Everlasting Message of Purpose & Grace
Enabling me to produce my fruit in my season
Over and over again.

If I have something to do for God
Will He not provide me the strength?
Will He not protect what He has invested?
Will He NOT provide unlimitedly for me?
Regardless to what it appears to be right now?
Regardless of the fact that I am Black

Lack has no power over a woman who obeys His voice.
God is no respect of persons, race or ethnicity
He is a respecter of those who walk by faith
And I believe Him, regardless to what you see
It's not about what you see, nor what you know
but all about what He said to me.
So be silent, be still and know
That He, not you…is God.

To Jesus, With Love

Jesus
I am so needy for you.
I have no one else and I feel so by myself.
I have so much to do
And I'm all alone
And I need you

I NEED YOU!

You are the drink that satisfies my thirsty soul
YOU are the pleasure I find, after I've been looking hard for so long
You warm my soul and make it sing Your Praises
You are the Comforter Who pleases me
You understand me, as I am
And You Love me... as I am
But You in Infinite Love will not let me remain that way
Because You have so much better for me
Than I could ever plan for myself.

So, take my hand, my Jesus
(Singing... Jesus, Lover of My Soul...)
I'll not fight Your way anymore
(Jesus... I will Never let You go...)
I'm tired and I'm lonely
(You've taken me... from the miry clay...)
I just want to go home
(You set my feet upon a rock... and now I know...)

All I want, all I need
(I love You... I need YOU...)
Is You.
(though my world may fall, I'll never let you go...)
No more, I need to roam.
(My Saviour... My Closest Friend...
I will worship You until the very end.)
Amen.

My Heart's Cry – For Truth

Here I sit
Been sitting for a while
Don't feel much like smilin'
Want to talk this out
but who will truly listen with an unbiased heart?
I feel bruised and really broken
Does anybody really care?
(Not if it's not convenient for them.)

Don't feel much like
Playin games with people anymore
Those who decide not to talk to me
I have very little tolerance for
I just really don't care anymore
This thing is really serious
And I have no more time to waste
Trying to please the unpleasable.

I mean, if you can walk away
Was your love truly real toward me in the first place?

I just want to sit and be still
And wait for God to talk
To ME.
Because all other voices proved faulty,
Even my own.

So, I don't need no opinions anymore

No coulda, shoulda, wouldas
No you ought tos, and
definitely not the how could you's
You can keep all of those to yourself
You do not know how this feels…To me
Because you were not there…
when I froze
when I fell
when the lights went out
Yours was not the name I called on
In the darkness of my night
Yours provided no assurance that you would hear and
answer my heart's cry
So why the hell would I want to hear what you have to say to
me now
When my heart, the core of who I am is full of matter
you've overlooked me and ignored the things I care about so
many times.
So I've learned NOT to ask you anymore.

I do not need your pat answers
Nor your tired religious clichés
full of nonsense and erroneous opinions about what you (on
the outside looking in)
think I should do with my life,
which is a life that is honestly not yours to live
and you give me advice so freely
that has led me nowhere, fast
this is something that I no longer want or need anymore
Right now, Today I need… the TRUTH.
The Word that has made me free!
Because now I understand, for the first time,

that I'll never find that I am looking for
depending upon You.
It's Jesus. Just Jesus
Is what I need to set my whole trust upon
Only Jesus. Just Jesus that I need
Only Jesus right now that I will wait for.

So if you can't give me Jesus
through the words you speak to me
Then please walk away and leave me be
for now, I am seeking the King
and I'll seek HIM
until the warm wind of His Spirit blows
Onto my ears, then deep inside my heart
causing both to open up and become aligned
To where I hear only His voice. HIS voice. HIS VOICE.
Where I can rise up on MY own two feet and walk
Stable and secure
Making straight paths for my feet
And fulfill my divine assignment in this world
Without the need that fuels me seeking your permission
Because my priorities are in order
my needs are met
(for real, this time)
and I'm accomplishing the things
that are pleasing to Him.
Living a life that I can approve
If you can't help me with that
Then get the hell away from me.
In Jesus' name, Amen.

Whatever happened to...

Whatever happened
To courtesy?

How did it become alright to
just "go off" because you've had a bad day
Over something, you THINK I've said?
Why do you feel that
Communication has occurred just because
I jump whenever you raise your voice
And I just "take it"
Because it will make me tougher
Whatever happened to
LOVE?

Is it EVER okay
Just to talk to each other
And breathe heart to heart?
How did it get to the place where because I do my job
We can't be friends anymore?
I'm so tired of fighting
Of being on edge ALL the time.
Don't touch this, bettah not bother that.
That's not yours, uh uhn, Don't miss that call…
And when you make a mistake
You're undone.

Whatever happened to…
I forgive you?

How did it become the way
To just beat each other up with our words
To talk to each other the way we do
It's so absurd.
The fact that we continue to do it, so insane.
Have we become so common
So used to doing what we do
That we forget there's SomeOne Else inside
Who hears and sees everything that we do?

Whatever happened to…
Handle with Care?

I don't feel like
Putting up my dukes and fight, anymore
I don't feel like keeping up my guardrails around you
tonight, anymore
I just…. Want… to… Be loved
Just to get along, this time,
For us to truly be on the SAME team
And to treat each other
with the love and respect
in the way that we say we would want.

Whatever happened to… LOVE?

How did it get to this?
Where because you know me
You think its alright to come at me

And speak to me the way you do
Just say anything, it's just Crystal, you know
And I'm supposed to just accept it
because it's you
And then, because I know you
I turn around (just as guilty) and I treat you with the same
condescension that I've had done
To me... Whaaat!?! When?
How did that become the way we do business:
To jump on each other when things don't go our way?

And how does this honor God
When I dishonor you
Ignoring your requests
Because I'm too busy with my own things to do?
Information is mishandled
because we don't communicate
We talk AT each other
With disgust and disdain

But we fail to talk with each other, TO each other
And then wonder why we miss making money that day
My God, is that how this must be?
We're running around like a car with old oil
Grinding on each other's nerves
Because it's what we've always done.
But that's NOT the way it should be
And I, for one, have had enough.

Please dear Jesus
Bring us back to our first love.

You can begin here
With me. Right here at the heart of the matter
Wash out my heart
From the soot of this day.
Cleanse Thou me from me
and from My funky attitudes
that have contributed to this way.
And when you're through
Grace me with the Almighty power of Your tender love
Oh yes, just refill me, refine me, renew me
Then please re-Grace me with the power of Your love.
So that I am peaceful, gentle, easy to be entreated
Full of mercy, and fruits that are borne from Above.
Dear Jesus, I pray.

Amen.

Impossible: A job for Superman

Impossibility is the opportunity
to let God handle the things
that are beyond your ability
to change, fix or do anything about.

Impossible means
That you've reached the end of your resources,
Your forces, your intelligence, your ingenuity and your capacity
are simply not enough
You've tried and you've finagled,
And you've gone as far as you could
You've even manipulated
You've put on your best dress
And your high heels
Your makeups on just right
Your hair is at its level best, honey
But yet and still, no one seemed to notice You.
And over many years nothing has changed
At least it seems that way to you

You've asked, you've begged and you've pleaded
But the answer remains the same.
You've knocked on so many doors
Everyone can see your hand's imprint in the frame
When they see you, they know what's coming
And so, they beat
A hasty retreat from you
But this is not the time for you to run and hide

Throw up your hands, toss in the towel and quit
For its times like these that are the signal
That this is a job for a Superman
An opportunity for the Almighty God to do His thing
And a sign that all you have to do in this
Is to keep… moving… forward

No! It's not the time for you to
"step back and let God do it…" alone
It's not the time for you to cry
"LORD, Do it! Lord, Do it for me…"
Instead, THIS is the time for you to marshal up your inner man
Keep on believing and take your stand
Keep showing up
Even when you're empty
Keep appearing…hopeful
Even when all hope is gone
Keep on believing and being your most beautiful you
Even when you are your least attractive self

For that's the point when the Word in you
Can work through you
To accomplish what you alone could never do
Your movement makes Him move
By His spirit operating through
The works of YOUR own hands

That's what turns impossibilities
Into manifestations of His victory
Over and over again.

Impossible is NOTHING
But an opportunity for God.
So, show up in whatever state you find yourself
resting assured that your God will indeed show out
just for you.

Then he said to me, "This is the word of the LORD to Zerubbabel saying, 'Not by might nor by power, but by My Spirit,' says the LORD of hosts. What are you, O great mountain? Before Zerubbabel you will become a plain; and he will bring forth the top stone with shouts of "Grace, grace to it!"'" Zech 4:6-7

*My lover took me to the wine house;
his intent toward me was love.*
Song of Solomon 2:4 Easy to Read Version

My Heart's Cry – For Wisdom

I've stumbled through
My whole life
Dependent
upon knowledge that came by trial and error
I simply didn't know
I didn't know what I needed to
To survive
Nor to thrive
My whole life was spent
Living on the winds of influence and advice
That came from this one and that one
The bite size nuggets of opinion, and yes, sometimes wisdom
From unreliable sources who
Were never around to pick up the broken and shattered pieces of
my heart, my llife
The fallouts from my decisions
Only God

I learned not to listen
I learned to give only an appearance of hearing
But relying on my own understanding (which wasn't much)
Acquired by lessons learned from falling over and over again
Lessons that left bruises and scars
Lessons that taught me well
What didn't work
But never instructing me on what really did
Until God

I grew in height and in stature
But never in mental acuity nor in much needed understanding
Just because I was physically "grown"

People assumed I knew
And treated me like I was a fool when I proved that I didn't know
as much as they thought I should
Little did they know
That I truly didn't
And so, I had to step up to life
And fill shoes that I never really got the point of how to wear them
The lessons I learned were very scary
I learned by trial of tasting this and sampling that
Only to wind up eating rocks and gravel
And dirt and empty hearts and pockets
The fruit of my own way
The way I asked for at age 10 when I told my mother "don't tell me
nothing, let me learn it for myself"
I swear to this day,
I don't know why I said that
Nor do I understand why, to me, she listened.
I guess God knows And understands it all.

But now...
Though I sit in "darkness" with empty pockets,
even though I went to work
my heart bursts open
Spilling out the blood of sorrow and grief
over the way I've run my life.
With much "intelligence" that I do have
That which people esteem so high and are even envious of –

I still lack the wisdom I that I need
To consistently bring forth the fruits thereof
The fruits of MY righteousness, borne and bred of God
Handicapped and cuffed by the fear that comes EV-ER-Y time that I
have to make a decision
Because I never understood how to make the right ones
Because now, right now, the older I get,
the consequences of these decisions are much more serious
They have devastating effects (or beneficial ones) upon the state of
my life and living conditions
Than they did when I was little
Depending upon the choice that I make,
is the food of which I must partake
Either good, or evil, or of God
So, I try so hard NOT to make any
Even though life itself demands that I must
So then, when I ask others what I should and should not do
Most look at me, like what are you asking me for?
And others who tell me
mostly base it upon their own opinion
fueled by what they think they know of me
Only one gives me instruction
based on the wisdom that comes from God
Who really gets and knows all about me
The man of God
Over the years I've heard so much

But did I truly listen?

Now, I sit
The present at a precipice
My time now where my voice is silenced
I have nothing more to say
Because it's time for manifesting
And I just cannot take another failed mission
Because I did things my own way
My (life, will, everything) is crumbled
My heart is set to hear from You
I need to hear the voice that gives instruction without beating me
over the head with opinion
and judgment.
I need to hear
From God.
From my man of God.
My ear presses upon every word
Looking right foolish, maybe even absurd
But I don't care
Just let me be found hearing and hearing The Word

The Demand to a Risen Savior from a Wounded Soul

Was I labeled as a child?
Or was strong willed what I really was?
Mom had me very young, I get that
A child became a mother through rape, from what I was told
Probably didn't know what to do with me
I get that too.
But was I really what you said that I was
Or was it only what you thought I was, in your eyes clouded by
your own agony and pain
you raised me and did the best you knew to do (I guess)
But did you ever try to "get" me?
Talk to me to try to understand
at least what, in my experience, was going on

Did you allow me to be myself
so I could bond with my identity
and learn the truth of just WHO I was
Did you even try to teach me about
the things that I NEEDED to know
about men
So I could learn how to handle my world? NO!
All you did was cuss at me and beat me
out of your own anger
over and over and over and over and over and over again

Never showed up for me, when the bullies at school attacked
Never showed up for anything I did
Never showed up for me at all.
Instead you let me experience the world
without knowing what to do
All on my own

Father, how do I handle the wounds within?
How do I cooperate with You to heal?
I wasn't expecting the reactions that rose up from inside
When faced with a past I hate
The panic attacks that happen when
faced with the things that I need so badly to erase
the things that scripture tells me to forget,
was told by wisdom to forget,
but yet and still I get reminded of them

Can anyone around me see? Better yet, do they even understand?
Instead it's mistaken for rebellion, the unplanned expression of
deep wounds within that I yet have to be healed
so that I can overcome the outward reactions of them.
They never ask me. They just judge me.
And assume they know the truth… all about me
Even though they surround me
They don't seek to get to the source of it all
And yet, I'm supposed to remain in control of my emotions
Don't "overreact" just simply comply
Doesn't matter the reasons why.

The many wounds that are gaping inside that I CAN FEEL
But everyone else denies the experience of.
I try to not show it,
Instead, I talk it all out with my Father
And I believe deep inside that HE understands me
He gets where I am and is moving me forward
by the lovingkindness of His spoken Word
He talks to me, and teaches me
And shows me that I am truly His own
He handles me as though I am treasured
And empowers me to do things that I've never done before
But those I must face every day do not see this
All they focus on are the things that I missed

All they see is the same old Miss.
And my wounds get reopened over and over again

Talk about craving You, Father?
I NEED You like I need every breath I take.
It is You Father, Who filled up my core
It was YOU Heavenly Father who closed up that deep gaping hole
I had within me
So now, I pray to You, my Heavenly Father
And respectfully place a demand upon Thee
to empower me to overcome the things that break me down
I cry out to you to Help me to heal INTERNALLY!!
There is no way that I can do this
without Your MIGHTY power.
Father, I am willing to work with You
I am willing to see this whole thing through
I am willing to overcome the scars that only You can see
The wounds that still rise up in anger and panic
and scream out of the deepest pain
Leave me the fuck ALONE!

Have mercy on me, my Heavenly Father
While everyone is talking about my physical body,
My deepest core is crying out to You, The Lord,
my Jehovah Shammah,
the One Who hears and sees and knows me well
Cover me up with Yourself, my Abba
Reach real down deep within and Heal my SOUL
I DO believe You, that my body is healed
But my body, to me, is NOT the problem.
It's the wounds nobody sees that are reopened and bleeding
Pour Your healing balm upon THEM
The wounds that seem to be unnoticed and ignored
The effects of which I cannot deny

I cry out to YOU, my Holy Advocate.
The one I KNOW is the Great Physician

I call on Your name to reach down within me and heal
Take away the pain deep within
bind up the scars that only YOU see
And then empower me to learn well
from YOU the things I feel I should have learned
when I was a child

Oh Lord, please know that I'm willing
Teach me once again, my Father,
the proper way, the RIGHT way to relate to others
And still be able to use my boundaries RIGHTLY
To be a better steward over my soul
then show me please, my Lord and Savior
the RIGHT way to relate to a man,
because no one ever taught me

Can you understand what I'm saying, Dear Father?
Can you enable the right ones to see?
Can you open the eyes of the blind to notice me
And be YOUR hands and eyes to take notice of
the wounds within that most ignore
I am willing to be used as a Healing balm to others
But I must be made whole first

So please my Father, answer me
For my life is in YOUR hands.
I believe that as this process happens
My body, I am confident, will recover and I, as YOUR woman will
be made completely whole
The only way I know to heal is to bring these wounds to light
I'm not asking for attention, like some people think
I'm simply asking to be made whole.

And she came to the place where she had been brought up: and, as her custom was, she went into the Lord's House on a Sunday, and stood up for to read. And there was delivered unto her the book of the prophet Esaias. And when she had opened the book, she found the place where it was written,

*"The Spirit of the Lord from my Pastor, Dr. Rickey Singleton is upon me, because he hath anointed **me** to preach the gospel to the poor; he hath sent me to heal the brokenhearted, to preach deliverance to the captives, and recovering of sight to the blind, to set at liberty them that are bruised, to preach the acceptable year of the Lord."*

And she closed the book, and she gave it again to the minister, and sat down. And the eyes of all them that were in the synagogue were fastened on her. And she began to say unto them,

This day is this scripture fulfilled in your ears.

Luke 4:16-21

Love Loves the Prodigal One

Just because you made a lot of mistakes
Can't keep you from returning to the love that you once knew
With a blessed assurance that He still wants you, too
That mess that you're in, is not endless (you're not hopeless)
In spite of what others say about you
Your frailties and failures won't disqualify you
from return to the one who loves you so
The One who gave up His life to redeem you too
Who's love's outstretched
For you, for you.

Just because the elder brother's jealous
It didn't stop the prodigal one from coming home
And it shouldn't stop you
Just because he squandered all he had and slept with pigs
Didn't keep him from remembering he was a son of a King

Love loves the prodigal one
Without limitations, terms or conditions
Love loves the prodigal one
Who comes back to his senses and comes
When you turn from that which led you astray
And to your heavenly Father you pray
The minute you take your first step in the right direction
Love runs your way

Just because you tumbled and took a hard fall
The mud on your face won't keep you from the right to call
On the name of the One who loves you most of all

Return to the house of the One
whose been calling on you, on you

ignore the looks on others faces
and come home

Love loves the prodigal one
Without limitations, terms or conditions
Love loves the prodigal one
Who comes back to his senses and returns
Just because others won't forget
Doesn't mean you have to live your life
In a sea of regret
Your Father promised, your sin He'd forget
Love loves the prodigal one
Love loves the prodigal one

Doesn't matter how many times you've fallen
Your redemption is sure
And so is the Father's call
For you to return
to the bosom of the only righteous One
Who redeemed us all
Your sinfulness won't keep you
And neither will your regret
Over the things that you did do
But God's not looking at that
His looking at His purpose in making you
No matter what the people say
They can't take your redemption away
So don't let them keep you from
entrusting your well-being to Him

As you return and partake of Your Father's ever present grace

So get up out of your sea of sorrow
And wipe the tears from your face
Just take that next right step
Come to the house of Grace
The place where you'll feel loved and wanted
And discover that you do belong and as you enter, be assured
that you will find
Your Father God will meet you where you are
You'll see that nothing couldn't separate you from His love
Because Love loves the prodigal one

and when you return, you will find
you're no longer the prodigal, you're still His son restored
and then you'll tell others that you know that
Love loves the prodigal one

Love loves the prodigal one
Love loves the prodigal one

Love loves the prodigal one
Love loves the prodigal one

It Happened One Night

Everything changed.
With one word. One night
The Word of the Lord came
Through the mouth of a Holy man
And My life has been transformed to where
I am now who I am
Born to be
Supposed to be
The soul thieves are gone.
The screaming inside has ceased.
Psychology didn't do this
So it cannot take the credit
Only God could put together
Something, someone who was broken to begin with

It was those who didn't know what to do with
The me that God created
That created the madness
The sadness that I had no choice but to walk through
But God
Was the One who saw me through each phase
And in One night, with one Wind of His Spirit
ended all the craziness
The madness and the sadness
The questions I thought would never be answered
not only were answered
but the need to ask any further questions
That night was stilled

I sit here more alive now
Than I ever have been in 55 years.

My questions all were answered
With just one word.
In One day and one night
It happened...
My little girl was found
And there was NEVER nothing wrong with her
Instead she's found her home
Deep Inside of me
Where she belonged before God
All along.

And I discovered... me.
I am black.
I am beautiful.
I am loved.
I am wanted.
And I am alive
Living for God's purpose
And they
The soul thieves of my soul,
the Me, I never knew 'til now are dead.
Their shit is done
And it was NEVER my fault.

It is over.
The burden of condemnation
DONE.

No more wondering
Wandering
Trying to be
Something I never was supposed to be in the first place

I'm free
To be ME.
And so I sit.
Breathing
Dreaming
Thinking
Planning
Walking
step by step in step with my Creator
walking by His faith
and now by His sight.

I am FREE!!
And NO ONE can ever take this away from me.
Forever and ever
AMEN!!

Your Face of Grace

In the quiet of the morning, I arise
Appreciative of your graciousness that saw me through
Providing for me by the way You've made for me
To do well, in places where before I once fell short
I thank You.

Money from my labor fills my bosom
Appreciative because now my needs are met
But there's a restlessness in my heart deep below
A sadness in my soul that my smiles before men
just won't erase
Because deep inside I know
I haven't completed the Work that will bring You glory
I need so bad to find pleasure once again within
Your face of Grace
It's not going to be the same before You until I do.

I want Your pleasure, Lord
In spite of all the kudos and accolades that surround me
I know it's all because of You.
Empowering me, anointing my mind
To do the things I do
Though my voice is the one speaking,
my hands that perform the work
It's only You, my Glorious Redeemer,
is the One who's shining through
And that's cool.
But still, I miss You, my Father

I miss the joy I found in pleasing You
Your face, the One shining brightly on mine
Making it glow with joy unspeakable
Your voice falling on my ears, telling me
"Daughter, I Am…so very proud of you."
No matter what I receive because I am working,
It's just not the same without You.

Abba Father, You are the Only Thing I really need
All that I have right now,
I know it can just as easily pass away,
People's accolades and kudos, I know too well
can just as easily turn away
And, I remind myself of that, so that I'll never forget
Your face of Grace
and use the gift of Your present provision
responsibly, as a tool
Ever mindful that I've GOT to complete
the things You want me to
For me, it just won't be the same until I do.

The Arrival

Well, here we are.
A new phase of a destined journey, I've begun
Walking in step with the Spirit, at long last
We've arrived, You and I
At the beginning of the journey into destiny.
And I'm so glad to share it with you…

But Jesus, It's YOU
Who is my Beginning and End
And everything in between
It is YOU - The One Constant in my life
It is YOU
At the beginning of each day and at day's ending
It's YOU - inside the love of anyone who loves me
It is YOU that's the fuel contained inside it
It is YOU Who remains, when they decide to leave
Or change toward me, or to love another,
It is YOU Who picks up the broken pieces
And repairs my broken soul again and again
Mending the cracks and crevices
And making me whole again and again
Making me willing to love again

It's YOU, it's YOU, it's YOU
The Lover of my soul
Who knows me better than about myself, I know
And yet… chooses to love me anyway
Again and again and again
All because it is a part of Your master plan - I'll TAKE it!
'Cause I belong to the GREAT I AM
I have arrived

So, here we are.
Step one of a destined journey, I've begun
Walking in step with the Spirit,
at long last We have arrived
At the beginning of the journey into destiny.
And I'm so glad to share it with You
Jesus.

Believe Again

You've done all
you've known to do
Falling again, upon your face – you blew it
Everyone knows your story
And they can tell it better than you
Or so they think
Yet in spite of all the shame
Going past the point of the deepest pain
Grace is there
That word once spoken
Still beats within
So Believe again
Believe again

Close your eyes
but not your ears
Let your bruised and broken heart be still
And Listen, as deep within, you'll hear
it bring back to your remembrance
All that God has said
to you

Believe again
Receive again

The dream
That seems so far away
Has not died, nor went away
Let God speak it to you again
Empowering you to rise again

wipe away the dust of shame
and take that tiny step of trusting Him
Believe on Him
Believe on Him

Close your eyes to what you see
Close off your mind
to what people have said
Walk away, if you must
But don't be scared
Be still and know that HE is God
Let the voice of God
Restore your trust
And believe again
Believe again

Close your eyes but not your ears
Let your bruised and broken heart receive
The word His voice speaks to you now
The word He spoke
when none of your critics were around
Let that voice of God breathe it into you again
'cause that's the only word you need to hear
it will lift you from the ground
So you can rise up and become
what God has destined you to be
'cause only He knows
who you truly are – in Him

So Believe again, Believe again
Receive His breath
And breathe it in
Believe again, Believe again

Let the Lord of love
Through the voice of God above
Breathe back into you His Grace
And take that tiny step of faith
It's time for you to hear one voice
With EVERY step you take
Stop looking at the winds and waves
Shut off the mouths of those who have so much to say
and believe again

Believe again.

Love in the Dance

I feel like dancing... Like old school modern dance
like I did back in High School
to songs that make me dream of things impossible
coming true
I dance, like no one's watching
doesn't matter what it looks like
'cause it's love coming straight from my heart
Let me dance... doesn't matter who sees me
let the music please me, comfort me
love me back to life
old school soul, pop power ballads
soft and soulful rock, like Sade and Jill Scott
if the music's right, it's all about love
the purity of which is determined by the sender
better check how you receive it, 'cause
it doesn't have to be religious, if the intent is right

let me dance to the music I hear
all through this night
because I believe in love
no matter how I express it
tonight, I unleash it at home unashamed
the cane doesn't matter
the weight's not a hindrance and
neither is my brace

I'll dance the way I want to tonight
'cause it's for no one in particular
but my dance showers love
for those close to my heart
expressed in the quiet movements before my Loving Lord
Out from my soul that's now open and transparent
before the God Who understands my way
of expressing pure love

in the dance.

For comments or requests for interviews or more, please contact me at

Crystal M. Gaines
CryGain Publishing House, LLC
15306 S. Robey Avenue, Suite 1301
Harvey, IL 60426
405-659-8748

Thank you for your support as
The Journey Continues!